"After reading *Dying to Meet Jesus*, you'l
Kay personally. He shares his experiences
ity and explains how, in the face of imper
Jesus in the most amazing way! Not only
his story also imparts a deeper revelation o... ...
never leave us or forsake us. In the midst of heartache, pain and suffering, Jesus is right there! I believe every reader will be able to relate
to Randy's story on some level. The insight shared in this book will
provide answers, supernatural strength and encouragement to those
walking through life's valleys."

Daniel Kolenda, president and CEO, Christ for all Nations

"I have one word for this book: *transformational*. Randy Kay's story-
telling and insights are extraordinary, with outstanding analysis and
reasoning, spot-on examples of how God answers prayer, portrayed
in a way that is so insightful it manages to make readers both challenged and comforted at once. In *Dying to Meet Jesus*, Kay finally
explains how we can draw closer to God as He uses brokenness to
draw us closer to Him. It all adds up to one compelling book that
carries tremendous weight."

Tommy Barnett, co-pastor, Dream City Church, Phoenix;
co-founder, Dream Center, Los Angeles and New York

"Suffering and brokenness can be God's means to melt, mold and
use His people. Mr. Randy Kay is one example of how God calls us
through difficulties in our lives. His near-death experience led him
to the place where he met Jesus, and this meeting with Jesus brought
many miracles upon his life. In this marvelous book, Mr. Kay shares
his story both from a clinical point of view about what it means to
heal and die and from a faith perspective about how God miraculously
heals people. I pray that our heavenly Father guides and blesses all
who read this wonderful book."

Young Hoon Lee, Ph.D., senior pastor, Yoido
Full Gospel Church, Seoul, South Korea

"In *Dying to Meet Jesus* Randy Kay shares heartbreaking stories, most
of them from his own personal experience, and reveals the secret for
turning pain and sadness into purpose and joy. My reaction can be
summed up in one word—WOW! God's miracles within these pages
will uplift you. The stories of suffering will actually encourage you.
You will catch a glimpse of heaven that very few have experienced

and returned to share. Randy Kay makes the revelation very personal and heartening. The journey within this book's pages will transform, inspire, motivate and encourage."

Rich Marshall, author and television host, God@Work

"Randy's honesty, insights and courage in expressing Christ's love through his and others' sufferings, as well as the intellectual force whereby he confronted his agnosticism in becoming an ardent follower of Christ, will inspire you. His transparent writing shows the centrality of brokenness in developing intimacy with Jesus—and subsequently joy—making *Dying to Meet Jesus* especially valuable to everyone seeking greater intimacy with God. Randy expresses the heart of Christ in a compassionate way few can deny."

Dr. Jim Garlow, *New York Times* bestselling author; former senior pastor, Skyline Church, San Diego; founder and CEO, Well Versed, Inc.

"In this revelational book, Randy Kay passionately guides us through the treacherous waters of overwhelming personal, physical and mental pain into the loving arms of Jesus. Through his excruciating journeys through multiple diseases and near-death experiences, Randy boldly shares his innermost struggles to poignantly proclaim that the presence of Jesus overcomes any suffering. God's amazing grace powerfully permeates every page of this powerful, uncompromisingly bold declaration of faith, fortitude and victory. A modern-day classic."

Dr. Jim Harris, executive advisor; international speaker; author, *Our Unfair Advantage: Unleash the Power of the Holy Spirit in Your Business*

"Randy Kay was an intellectual cynic who experienced one of the most profound God encounters I have ever heard in my life. In *Dying to Meet Jesus*, Randy has articulated his life of brokenness from deep pain on multiple unexpected levels from a view of intimacy with Father God that is refreshing to my heart and groundbreaking in truth. Randy became a friend to my heart as he helped me see the value of pain in my journey of destiny from a different aspect. This is a book you will want to give to your friends."

Dale L. Mast, senior pastor, Destiny Christian Church, Dover, Del.; author, *And David Perceived He Was King*, *Two Sons and a Father* and *The Throne of David*

"Randy Kay shares in a transparent, practical and inspiring way that trials and tribulations (even to the point of near death) aren't our enemies but, as James 1:2–4 says, our friends. He shows that they aren't to be rejected but embraced, and teaches us not to ask, 'Why is this happening to me?' but, 'What can I learn from this?' And then he shows the great reason—we can become complete and whole as we meet and fall in love with Jesus. Thanks, Randy, for touching our lives so profoundly by learning how to turn our sorrow into joy and our pain into purpose."

Dr. Ron Jenson, "America's Life Coach"; co-founder, Future Achievement International; founder and chairman, High Ground

"Thank you, Randy, for this transparent account of your progressive intimate journey with God. This book inspires and instructs while laying a framework to have our own encounters with the Lord. Randy's statement that 'experiencing God is more about relationship than it is about faith' is a reminder of God's heart toward us. *Dying to Meet Jesus* shows us that finding God in adversity aligns us to our assignment. This places us within the grace zone of our redemptive purpose and releases many natural and spiritual gifts as we experience an outpouring of His love. This is a well-written, inspirational read."

Gary W. Carter, founder and lead pastor, Life Church, Drayton Valley, Alberta; founder, Transitional Leadership training program

"Randy's personal near-death experience provides stunning evidence that indeed, 'The LORD is close to the brokenhearted and saves those who are crushed in spirit' (Psalm 34:18). Randy's insights into how God uses our brokenness to conform us to His image are practical and compelling. Don't miss the opportunity to grow deeper in your relationship with Jesus by yearning for, and experiencing, His presence now in your life. Let *Dying to Meet Jesus* lead you into a stronger and more joyful walk with Jesus Christ."

Dr. Larry A. Vold, associate pastor, 3 Crosses Church, Castro Valley, Calif.; author, *The Good Fight: Spiritual Warfare and the Believer's Hope*

"Randy Kay is a logical, analytical, scientific thinker who does not lend himself to wild speculation or fanciful imaginations. Part of the credibility of his story is that he is one of the last people on earth one would expect to have such a story. Randy's book delves into the depths of human suffering and disappointment. How we hold on to the hand of Jesus when life itself is full of pain is one of the greatest secrets of Christian living. Randy's journey through the valley of the shadow of death is an inspiration and comfort to us all."

Rob Bryceson, lead pastor, The Gathering House,
Spokane, Wash.; co-founder, Street Wise Ministries;
author, *Lessons from a Church in Zombie Land*

"I am deeply grateful to Randy Kay for writing this book. With personal and profound insight into suffering and loss, tragedy and the miraculous, Randy leads us to understand suffering's transformative power, creating a life force of depth, passion and intimacy with our Heavenly Father and others."

Sheri Briggs, founder, Bridge of Hope

"I have spoken with so many people who cannot make the connection between their troubles, suffering and pain and our Father's purpose for their lives. Compelling, compassionate, and comforting are the words that come to mind and heart after reading Randy's new book! *Dying to Meet Jesus* will transform your mind to think anew about brokenness, and God's love for you."

Thom Corrigan, author and business leader

"Transformational power lies within the pages of Randy Kay's *Dying to Meet Jesus*—power to bring hope to the brokenhearted and to stir up a hunger in readers to experience more of Jesus. The personal stories shared reveal the heart of Emmanuel—God with us—in the midst of painful life challenges and circumstances."

Shae Bynes, founder, Kingdom Driven Entrepreneur;
author, *Grace Over Grind: How Grace Will Take
Your Business Where Grinding Can't*

"I love the book! It is real! It is raw! It is honest! It is intimate! Don't miss reading *Dying to Meet Jesus*!"

Sheila Harden, Ph.D., radio host, *Coffee Break*

DYING
TO MEET
JESUS

DYING
TO MEET
JESUS

HOW ENCOUNTERING HEAVEN
CHANGED MY LIFE

RANDY KAY

Chosen

a division of Baker Publishing Group
Minneapolis, Minnesota

Published by Chosen Books
Minneapolis, Minnesota
www.chosenbooks.com

Chosen Books is a division of
Baker Publishing Group, Grand Rapids, Michigan

Printed in the United States of America

ISBN 978-0-8007-9950-2

Library of Congress Cataloging-in-Publication Control Number: 2019950004

Unless otherwise indicated, Scripture quotations are from the Holy Bible, New International Version®. NIV®. Copyright © 1973, 1978, 1984, 2011 by Biblica, Inc.™ Used by permission of Zondervan. All rights reserved worldwide. www.zondervan.com. The "NIV" and "New International Version" are trademarks registered in the United States Patent and Trademark Office by Biblica, Inc.™

Scripture quotations identified ASV are from the American Standard Version.

Scripture quotations identified ESV are from The Holy Bible, English Standard Version® (ESV®), copyright © 2001 by Crossway, a publishing ministry of Good News Publishers. Used by permission. All rights reserved. ESV Text Edition: 2016

Scripture quotations identified HCSB are from the Holman Christian Standard Bible®, copyright © 1999, 2000, 2002, 2003, 2009 by Holman Bible Publishers. Used by permission. Holman Christian Standard Bible®, Holman CSB®, and HCSB® are federally registered trademarks of Holman Bible Publishers.

Scripture quotations identified NASB are from the New American Standard Bible® (NASB), copyright © 1960, 1962, 1963, 1968, 1971, 1972, 1973, 1975, 1977, 1995 by The Lockman Foundation. Used by permission. www.Lockman.org

Scripture quotations identified NHEB are from the New Heart English Bible.

Scripture quotations identified NKJV are from the New King James Version®. Copyright © 1982 by Thomas Nelson. Used by permission. All rights reserved.

Scripture quotations identified NLT are from the Holy Bible, New Living Translation, copyright © 1996, 2004, 2007, 2013, 2015 by Tyndale House Foundation. Used by permission of Tyndale House Publishers, Inc., Carol Stream, Illinois 60188. All rights reserved.

Scripture quotations identified NRSV are from the New Revised Standard Version of the Bible, copyright © 1989 National Council of the Churches of Christ in the United States of America. Used by permission. All rights reserved.

Cover design by Rob Williams, InsideOutCreativeArts

Author represented by Literary Management Group

Baker Publishing Group publications use paper produced from sustainable forestry practices and post-consumer waste whenever possible.

This book is dedicated
to all those in the midst of suffering.
You are loved more than you can
possibly comprehend. I know.

Contents

Foreword

Over the last thirty years, I have studied over one thousand cases of people who have clinically died yet revived. In some cases, their hearts stopped beating, even brainwaves had ceased, yet they were resuscitated and came back to declare the wonders of the life to come. What Randy shares of his own experience when a pulmonary embolism caused his clinical death (and Randy has proof he actually died) lines up with many of the commonalities of these near-death experiences I have studied. Millions have had similar experiences to Randy's. The Gallup Poll declared that 1 in 25 Americans has had a near-death experience. Yet just as Randy was hesitant to share his sacred time with Jesus, others find it difficult to talk about as well.

Imagine if our lives were being lived out on a flat, two-dimensional, black-and-white painting. Death is when your spirit separates from this life, so imagine your spirit torn off that flat painting and brought out into a three-dimensional room of color containing the black-and-white picture. Suddenly you come alive in new dimensions and experience colors you have never seen. From this new perspective, you can see your flat-painting world as a part of a bigger reality. Then imagine being "brought back" to two-dimensional life on that painting. How would you describe a third dimension of colors in two-dimensional, black-and-white words? I am convinced that is what people who have near-death experiences struggle to do— explain heaven's extradimensional reality in limited 3D words.

As a Christian pastor, my interest in near-death experiences is to understand how they line up with what the Bible has already revealed about the life to come, and to help people better know how to live life now in line with God's purpose. But I was once a skeptic and agnostic. I was not a believer when my dad was dying of cancer. A friend gave him the first book on this well-hidden, pervasive phenomenon, *Life After Life*. It was the book that coined the term "near-death experience." I read it in one night and thought, *Oh, my gosh, this God stuff and Jesus stuff may be real, and if so, it's the most important thing in life*. The next year, I joined a Bible study, where I came to faith in Jesus, understanding for the first time the free gift of forgiveness and eternal life offered by God's grace.

So after thirty years of studying the Bible, in seminary and as a pastor, and at the same time studying over one thousand of these near-death experiences, I wrote *Imagine Heaven* to show how these testimonies add color to the picture of the life to come already revealed in the Bible. And that is what I so appreciate about Randy's story and the biblical insights he shares. Randy's story aligns with many of the commonalities of the experiences I have studied, yet his journey is also unique in several ways.

First, sharing his story could cost Randy considerably. As Randy and I sat at lunch overlooking the pristine San Diego harbor near his home, he said to me and my son, "Publishing this book could be the end of my career. But I feel it's what God wants me to do." Randy writes about his encounter with Jesus in heaven while serving as the CEO of a successful company, which should not be taken lightly.

I have studied and interviewed doctors, professors, commercial airline pilots, bank presidents and others whose near-death experiences line up with Randy's story. What possible motivation could Randy or these people have for making up a wild tale of dying and seeing heaven, even meeting God? Why would successful professionals make up such similar stories? I can find no good reason, except it happened.

I was an engineer before becoming a pastor, so I am interested in the analytical evidence of heaven's reality that these modern-day medical miracles reveal. I believe they provide scientific evidence of the afterlife. The fact that Randy and many others do not need to make money from selling books, yet courageously write about their experiences despite how it could hurt their professional credibility, is powerful evidence.

It is fascinating that they all insist when they passed from this life, they came fully alive—more alive than they had ever felt before—not just with five senses, but alive with fifty senses, as many describe it. Like Randy, many traveled to a heavenly realm of beauty—not unlike earth, but earthlike beauty experienced in new dimensions of time and space. The mountains are more majestic, the flowers and trees and grass are more alive and vivid, the colors far surpass our color spectrum, and all are infused with the very glory and light of God—a light that is palpable love and life radiating out of everything. Many of these people met God on the other side, and in His presence, they experienced a love transcending all the individual experiences of love they had ever experienced on earth. Imagine feeling all those loves, at once, times one thousand!

At lunch, every time I asked Randy to describe what it felt like to be with Jesus, he struggled to find the words as he fought back overwhelming emotion. It was evident the love and joy he experienced is just as real to him today as it was then, and trying to describe the feeling left him speechless. Shifting subjects to gain composure, Randy described the immense beauty of this paradise surrounding him, which he details later in this book, but he kept saying, "Yet as spectacularly beautiful as paradise was, nothing compared to Him. He was all that mattered and all I wanted, and the intimacy and love I experienced made all other beauty and splendor pale in comparison."

My son and I left our lunch feeling as if we had gotten a sacred peek into the immense love that God has for each one of us, and we could not stop talking about it. I think you will get the same glimpse as you read Randy's story and spiritual insights.

Many of the people I studied indicated that before God sent them back, He would say something to the effect of, *You must go back. Your purpose is not yet completed.* What Randy shares surrounding this experience, especially regarding purpose in life, is profoundly important for our spiritual growth. I was so grateful I took my son along to join us at lunch that day. I knew that my son, a 22-year-old seeking to find and live out his purpose (as we all do), would be excited to hear what Jesus told Randy about discovering purpose in life. Randy's insight impacted my son greatly, as it did me, and will you, too, as you read his story.

The wisdom Randy received from Jesus does not add to the Bible, but it is unique in that it clarifies what the Bible teaches about how each one of us can follow the purpose God created us to live. That insight alone is worth the price of the book, and I hope you ponder deeply the wisdom Randy conveys about the purpose God put you here to accomplish. No matter where you have been, what you have done or what difficulties you may encounter in the future, God loves you more than you can imagine! He has a plan for your life, and you *can* succeed in finding and fulfilling His plan.

I also appreciate that Randy is a devoted follower of Jesus. Randy has been tested in every way, yet his faith has remained and grown stronger through it all. Not only will you be captivated by Randy's experience in the presence of Jesus, but you will be inspired and blessed by the scriptural wisdom and insight God has given him through the pain and suffering he has endured. I truly believe Randy's story will help you learn to navigate life's difficulties with a faith and a love that grow stronger through them all.

John Burkc, *New York Times* bestselling author, *Imagine Heaven*; founding pastor, Gateway Church, Austin

Acknowledgments

Renee, who held my hand in prayer the day we married, the day I nearly died, and all those days that included our trials for as long as it took to experience the joys through them.

My children, who have taught me about God's love and about His grace. You persevered through many challenges, and I am so very proud of you.

Rich Marshall, who unleashed my destiny in prayer and support as I started my human development firm, and encouraged me to share my story.

Bruce Barbour, my literary agent and friend, who saw in *Dying to Meet Jesus* the potential to portray God's love to others.

My friends at Chosen, who have invested their faith and efforts in bringing this book to those who need it.

Northwestern University for being my academic home as a student of writing and science while allowing me to research the world's religions as an agnostic, which served to validate my current faith in Christ.

Introduction

Doctors told me I am "lucky to be alive." I had been victimized by my greatest fear. My fear? Yes, I had been overcome with the fear that I would slowly suffocate to death, first as if I was sipping air through a cocktail straw for days until at last it felt as if duct tape had been strapped across my mouth. Beginning in childhood, I had suffered from asthma and as an adult from chronic obstructive pulmonary disease (COPD), so I knew firsthand the panic that usually sets in from not being able to breathe. At the point of desperation, you want to pass out but cannot. In that moment, with blood clots clogging my main airway, I gasped for breath, as if someone were pressing a pillow over my face relentlessly as I lay there waiting for death.

But the sad irony of my fight to live is that my fight with death was not my greatest struggle—not even close. Facing mental illness, the effects of drug abuse, personal losses and confusion as to why God seemed to turn a deaf ear to all of my trials caused me to feel alone, abandoned. My daughter suffered strokes, fell victim to drugs and tried to kill herself. My son inherited my depression. Troubles with our marriage and our finances led my wife and me to a point of looking at websites detailing how to commit suicide. But a crisis of faith caused me to challenge God to show up.

And wow, did He ever show up!

Nevertheless, it took brokenness to see God and to live out my purpose. That is what this book is about—finding purpose and intimacy with God through pain. Although readers may be fascinated by my encounter with Jesus during a near-death experience, the story did not end there. A trail of trials and miracles took me on a spiritual journey that I liken to hiking the "Death Trail" of Mount Huashan in China, which, for those of you who do not know about it, has been rated as one of the toughest treks in the world. Trust me when I tell you that the stories of my expedition that I share on these pages are stained with tears.

The journey to closeness with God is cluttered with broken shards that can pierce you to the point of almost giving up. Looking back, I would have preferred to walk a mile over broken glass than to have gone through the suffering of those I dearly love.

Maybe you have felt the same. Trials are the inevitable consequences of living in this world. But the reasons God permits us to go through them are more elusive. For now, I will just say there is a purpose through our pain, and as we journey through the pages of this book, we will look at why God not only allows brokenness but also requires it for a higher purpose than we could possibly understand while caught in the midst of adversity.

Helping people fulfill their purpose has consumed much of my life. After a thirty-year career in business, I founded a human development firm called PACEsetters (www.pacesetters .training) and have trained lots of people—almost one million, in fact, according to my team's most recent count. And as an ordained minister, I have taught numerous church classes across a broad range of biblical topics.

But now my most important purpose is focused on *you*, because you have honored me by reading the content of my heart within these pages. And I will share with you my humbling secret: My failings and my sufferings have allowed me to know God as my Friend and Counselor and to attain a level of success I could not possibly have achieved by anything this world offers. Before I got real with God, I was often faking it.

When the tough times happened, all too often I doubted the Lord. Only during the good times did my faith seem justified. In the back of my mind, I wondered, *Am I just imagining God's presence in my life?* Not now. I do not just hope that Jesus Christ is real; I have met Him face-to-face. And the steadfastness of my relationship with Him was inextricably strengthened not only in meeting him at the point of death but, to my surprise, through the hard times that followed. Jesus is more real to me today than most of the people I meet in this world. He is also greater than anyone can possibly imagine.

For a long time, I did not want to write this book for fear of the skepticism I myself used to feel after hearing others share similar accounts. I used to mock those claiming to have met God in near-death experiences. Besides, my journey of finding joy through suffering was just too personal, and I did not want to embarrass anyone whose story in this book reveals the rawness of the human condition.

Then came the interview on GodTV.

The host, my former pastor, asked me about my near-death experience on air. Previously, I had only shared my experience with close family and friends. Before the camera, not a hair was out of place, my shoes were shined, my T-shirt was even ironed, and the makeup lady had powdered my face three times. I was prepared with rehearsed answers to anticipated questions. But when I began to share my intimacy with Jesus in heaven, the mere memory caused me to cry like a two-year-old.

On the return flight from the interview, I stared at the peanut bag on my tray for about thirty minutes. My treasure was no longer just mine. People would think of me as a quack, or so I thought. That is when Jesus told me to write a book.

So I began writing, boasting of my accomplishments—you know, those achievements I felt were needed to establish my credentials that most of my training clients required in order to validate my writings and to qualify my coaching services.

No, God's Spirit told me, *I want you to write about your failures and your sufferings*. After several rewrites, He added, *And I want you to share our special time together*.

I teared up again. Really? Again? Never in my life had I written about my sufferings and losses. Never. And I wanted to tuck my heavenly meeting with Jesus back into its treasure chest.

God was pushing a story and a message out of me with the force of an oil gusher, and I feared the muck that might pour out. He reminded me of some of my most painful memories as a testimony that we can all survive, and even thrive, through life's trials.

That is how God inspired me to write *Dying to Meet Jesus*.

As I look back, these memories have framed my mission to help give hope to the hopeless. Indeed, the key to joy through sadness happens when we learn to unpack our hearts with memories so we can unleash our destiny.

I am writing from the perspective of someone in love with Jesus Christ, but I was not always a Christian. I have studied all the major religions and was a devoted agnostic in my youth. My passion now is to free people from the limited thinking that prevents them from realizing the fullness of their relationship in Christ. Part of that includes breaking the barriers that place religion over relationship.

Yes, heaven is for real—I have seen it. Yes, God is for real—I have seen Him, too. I became comatose and nearly died as my blood flow stopped, and I temporarily left this world. But it was not heaven that impressed me so much as it was being in the comforting embrace of Jesus. Someone could have thrown me in a dumpster, and I would have rejoiced if it meant being in there with Jesus. Come to think of it, one could say that this world is like living in a dumpster compared to the wonders of heaven, especially if you have lost someone, been disabled or rejected, or experienced a host of other terrible things that circle in this world like a vulture ready to pounce on someone's dying soul.

Most of my encounters with God are in pleasant heart-to-hearts (perhaps you can relate). But three times I have encountered the God of Love in a miraculous way. Each happened differently—one through searching for the truth, one through dying and one through intense worship. But I have always been with God, even when I did not know it. The same applies to you. God is with you even if you are not with Him. That is the conundrum of walking with Christ.

Know this: You are chosen. Your Father wants to keep you in His loving protection. Jesus desires a deeper place in your heart. The Holy Spirit wants to comfort you beyond the cares of this world. God will find you in your deepest sorrow, but He will never leave you there. Your destiny is the mountaintop over which you will see God's glory that cannot be described by any words in all the dialects of this world. And, believe me, you will be absolutely overwhelmed with God's goodness when you get there.

Three times in my life I have encountered a heavenly visitation with my Lord, the first being what Jesus explained in John 3:3 as being born again, meaning a conversion to a personal faith in Christ. Later, I will explain how I crossed the divide of my agnosticism in becoming a believer. My second transcendence followed my near-death experience (NDE) in heaven. That one was ineffable, but I will try to explain it for you. As He does with most believers, God almost always speaks to me in my conscience with a "gentle whisper" as explained in 1 Kings 19:12. Sometimes He opts to speak through others or directly through a sense of peace or even through a profound revelation. My third encounter happened during a Christian men's retreat in Tahoe, which revealed to me the difference between God the Father, the Son and the Holy Spirit. My NDE created a familiarity with Jesus that opened a window to experiencing God more deeply during that precious time. But more about that later in the book.

I wrote a novel as a cathartic way to express my time with Jesus. While writing this book, I would be awoken in the middle of the night to jot down insights from heaven—events in conversation with Christ. I now understand that my intimacy with Jesus stayed with me long after meeting Him, resulting in a spiritual awakening entirely new to me. The Holy Spirit would reveal conversations with Jesus I had experienced in heaven that lay dormant until God's Spirit refreshed my recollection. Our together times since the hospital encounter with my Savior have become as conversational as two intimate friends communing with each other. We now talk continuously with most of the language being in the form of peace and assurances. He always tells me this: *Trust me.* That does not come naturally for a "prove it" kind of guy like me.

This book begins with dying and ends with a celebration in heaven. You can decide whether to believe these stories or not. I simply want you to know that they have been verified clinically and through witnesses. As a trained professional in the healthcare industry, I have participated in surgeries, educated physicians on drug therapies and led clinical teams in cardiology and neurology. So I am writing to you from both a clinical perspective of what it means to heal and to die, as well as from a faith perspective. On numerous occasions, I have witnessed God healing people supernaturally. I will share some of these miracles with you, including several that defy human understanding.

In chapter 1, you will learn about my time with Jesus. The Holy Spirit released many of the details from my memory vault after I recovered enough to recollect the fullness of my experience. These include my conversations with Jesus about purpose and about life in general, including my observation about being in paradise with Jesus. I am not saving this part until the end as a teaser to get you to read this book. Rather, before you can realize the full measure of God's love, there is a journey we must take together. Please join me as we explore the unfathomable depth of Christ's love and God's destiny for each of us through life's inevitable peaks and valleys, before reaching our final destination in heaven.

—1—

Face-to-Face

About two years prior to my near-death experience (NDE), my employer, once the fastest-growing pharmaceutical company in the world, laid off almost all of its sales and marketing employees after a recall of a drug that was hailed as a probable "cure" for Alzheimer's. Only a few months before, I attended a meeting in Washington, D.C., to announce a new vaccine against Alzheimer's. We were on all the major networks—CNN, Fox News, NBC, CBS, ABC—and the front cover of *Time* magazine. I created a tagline for the introduction of our drug: Making Alzheimer's History. Finally, there was a cure for one of the most devastating diseases of all time.

With the final stage of clinical trials nearly complete, our company stock rose to record highs. Cashing in on my soon-to-vest stock would net me millions. I would be able to fulfill my dreams.

Then came the crash. A few patients in the trial suffered from encephalitis, an inflammation of the brain. This potentially fatal side effect led the FDA to force a recall of our drug. Soon after, a *Wall Street Journal* front-page story broke the news that our chief financial officer had used off-balance accounting to allow our company to acquire several other companies. Though this was legal, it appeared that our pharmaceutical company was "cooking the books."

Our stock price slid down faster than a greased pig on a fun slide. Within weeks, it became a penny stock. I had to lay off my entire department, and then the board laid me off. My job evaporated, and with it all of my pledged stock and the dreams therein. I would realize the ultimate loss only years later, when my mother developed Alzheimer's. I could only imagine how, if our drug had been made available, she might never have fallen into the cruel grip of this horrid disease.

After a brief tenure with another pharmaceutical company, I started a biotech company. But that venture fizzled when it was clear I needed to raise over sixty million dollars to keep the company afloat.

So I decided to acquire a newspaper. It seemed like God's next career move. I love writing, having studied journalism at Northwestern University, and envisioned growing the enterprise into a media conglomerate—maybe the next Viacom or Fox. Soon after spending much of my savings just to buy this company, I learned that the previous owner had overstated the number of committed advertisers. Turned out, many of the current advertisers intended to discontinue their advertising as soon as their contracts expired. Not wishing to invest another fortune to keep funding the newspaper, I closed the publication. It seemed I was on a slippery slope to nowhere with a young family to feed and a large mortgage to pay.

God, I prayed, *why did you allow me to go down this path?*

Bills continued to stack up. My wife cried at night. And I recall looking at our young children and worrying about their future. Thoughts of cashing in on my life insurance through a veiled suicide crossed my mind. Like George Bailey from that favorite Christmas movie, *It's a Wonderful Life*, I wondered if perhaps I was "worth more dead than alive."[1]

One night I stared at the ceiling and said, "God, this time You need to show up—I want to see You!"

My Brush with Death

One desperate evening in the spring of 2004, my wife, Renee, and I sat at a Christian coffee house in Escondido, California, lamenting our situation, drowning our sorrows in lattes. I recall saying, "Well, dear, at least we have our health." To relieve stress and give myself some semblance of success, I would exercise daily—cycling, weightlifting, running. In my forties, I rivaled the height of my youthful sports conditioning. So even if I was a mental wreck, I was still physically fit. Yep, at the very least we had our health.

Two days later, a recruiter called me from a company I had formerly worked for with much success, Johnson & Johnson (J&J), the largest healthcare company in the world. My former positions—sales manager, trainer, and marketing executive—bode well for gaining the open position to lead a clinical and sales team for the West. So the company flew me to New Jersey for a series of interviews.

The next day, after an apparently successful round of interviews, I flew back to San Diego. The next day, my right calf began to swell. I went to the gym, and then cycled up the coast. Later that day, each step shot pain through my leg. The next day, my calf had swelled to almost twice its size, a result of straining my muscle from exercising the day before, or so I reasoned. As the day progressed, I could not move my leg while walking up the stairs without feeling stinging pain up my leg and a dull heaviness in my calf.

Meanwhile, Renee and I continued planning our family trip to Joshua Tree National Park in a rented RV, a much-needed family vacation to decompress after months of stress. Nothing would deter me from granting our children their long-anticipated RV journey to the majestic mountains of California and Colorado. We had been talking about it for months.

That Friday, the hiring vice president at J&J called me. "We'd like to offer you the position," she said, "and we'll bridge your prior service with J&J."

I responded with a resounding yes while proclaiming a silent hallelujah. My drought would finally end. I hobbled down the stairs to share the good news with Renee. Everything seemed to be lining up for good, except for my excruciatingly painful and swollen leg.

Then my breathing worsened. My first thought was that I was experiencing the worst asthma attack of my life. But I did not freak out about it, suspecting that my seasonal asthma, due to pollen in the air and leaf molds, must have worsened because of my recent cycling routine. I pressed on, focused on the brighter future that awaited us.

Meanwhile, my energy level dropped. I would bend over to pick something up and become tired in the process. I struggled to catch my breath, inhaling deeply without any relief. Though this was very puzzling to me, I ignored it.

I reached down to pick up a small bag of kitchen trash that weighed no more than five pounds. I got maybe two or three steps and needed to stop from exhaustion. I waited a few seconds before continuing my twenty-foot journey to the trash area outside. Three, four steps later, same thing—exhaustion. Four puffs of my rescue inhaler did nothing to help.

"God, what's going on?"

Remembering our celebratory vacation, I put off a trip to the doctor just hoping I could endure the suffering. But when the pain forced me almost to a crawl, I decided to visit an orthopedist to get a prescription for a muscle relaxant and perhaps a painkiller. By now, I had lost the ability to bend my leg without feeling piercing stings up and down and having to take several puffs of my albuterol inhaler to catch my breath. It was double trouble—I could not walk or breathe. So once I got to the ortho-pedist, instead of giving me painkillers and a muscle relaxant, he rushed me to the nearest hospital emergency room.

They completed an ultrasound on my leg, then carted me back to the ER. The doctor came back with a worried look on his face and said, "You have elevated levels of D-dimer." For those of you who are unfamiliar with this term, D-dimer is a fibrin degradation product (or FDP), a small protein fragment present in the blood after a blood clot is degraded by fibrino-lysis. It is so named because it contains two D fragments of the fibrin protein joined by a cross-link. Elevated levels in my blood could have meant several things, none of them good.

I experienced all the symptoms of a pulmonary embolism, such as lack of oxygen that caused my strained breathing. A pulmonary embolism happens when a clot wedges itself in one of the pulmonary arteries or its branches. Pulmonary emboli can block the entire right or left pulmonary artery, stopping the blood flow to the entire lung—and causing death. So the doctors and nurses scurried to get an IV in my arm to start a heparin drip. Heparin is an anticoagulant intended to prevent blood cells from clotting.

A dull pain, like a pulled muscle, settled in my chest and back just under my left breast. But before long, it felt as if a three-hundred-pound man was sitting on my chest, and I la-bored to breathe as if something had placed a hand over my mouth. Panic surfaced. Staff began rotating in and out of my ER room. By then, my right calf appeared twice as big as the left one. I could not stand and could barely push any air in or out of my lungs.

A team unlocked my bed and ran me to radiology, where they placed me on a slab for a CT (computed tomography) scan. Shortly after, a respiratory therapist wedged a breathing apparatus into my mouth to force as much air as possible through my narrowed windpipe.

My heart began racing.

The nurse who took my vitals said I was a "walking dead man."

Then a physician came in and, with a furrowed eyebrow, informed me that I had six blood clots. "It's very serious," he added, "because the clots have traveled to your lungs and are blocking your pulmonary artery, the only passageway to your lungs." He told me I was one of the "lucky ones," because a lot of people in my condition who come into the hospital vertical leave horizontal, feet first.

Imagine how comforting those words were to me as I lay there in a panic, literally suffocating to death, as though I was being immersed in water and forced to stay there. Later, I would learn that a 27-year-old surfer died that night from the same critical illness I was experiencing, pulmonary embolism, which is the third leading cause of death. A victim can die within seconds.

My condition was in the advanced stage, as five major clots and one growing clot were almost completely occluding my only airway. The only immediate solution requires a specially trained surgeon with experience in performing an embolectomy (surgical removal of a blood clot). The surgeon would need to place me on cardiopulmonary bypass (so a machine could do the work of my heart and lungs), crack open my chest and adroitly reach in with a fine instrument to pierce the pulmonary artery and pull out the clots. None of those specialist surgeons lived within thirty miles of the hospital where I lay in mortal crisis. By the time the surgical team prepped me and the surgeon arrived, I would be dead.

In a crisis, near death, I learned that prayer turns into shouts of desperation. There is no time for casual requests. Screams to God rose silently from within my spirit. I thought of my children, little Ryan, ten, and Annie, eight, and my faithful wife, Renee, who just hours before had found some glimmer of hope because, finally, I would be going back to a well-paying job.

Renee had stopped working outside the home after our children were born. I knew that without me she would not be able to support the family in the lifestyle we were accustomed to. We had gone from living "the dream" in a million-dollar-plus house with an income in the top percentile of wage earners to having no insurance and being in the bottom percentile. And here I was facing death and hospital bills that would bankrupt my family.

God, why now? Why at the cusp of finding hope?

And then I thought back to my conversation with Renee at the coffee house. *At least we have our health*, I had said.

Not now. Even that was gone.

Then came the waiting.

My IV line was my only hope of surviving. Drip, drip, drip . . .

My eyes fixed on the slow flow of clear liquid intended to prevent further clotting. For two days, I labored to breathe with air pouring into my lungs through a ventilator. A second scan revealed that the blockage in my lungs occluded the pulmonary artery. Weakness forced me to sleep until I awoke gasping for air.

A doctor who came into my room to draw blood strained to get a drop of blood. "Strange," he said. "I can't draw any blood from your arm." He looked down and spotted some redness around the site where the IV needle entered my vein, then sent what little blood he could draw to the laboratory for analysis.

The result showed I had an infection caused by staphylococcus bacteria now surging throughout my bloodstream because the infection had passed through the IV line. Further lab results confirmed the infection as methicillin-resistant staphylococcus aureus (MRSA), which is caused by a type of staph bacteria that has become resistant to many of the antibiotics used to treat ordinary staph infections. My strain happened to be one of the most resistant strains, and my body was in severe sepsis with the next stage being septic shock. The MRSA, having been carried on the tip of my IV needle into the vein, now surged throughout my body, threatening to shut down one or more of my organs.

Now I had two of the top "killers" attacking my body, along with the threat of pneumonia because of my compromised lungs. The infection continued coursing through my entire body. This final attack created hypercoagulability throughout my bloodstream such that my blood cells formed a series of clumps that blocked the passage of other blood cells. It was like a series of car accidents blocking movement on dozens of roadways, or veins and arteries in this case. One of the physicians explained that if one of the blood clot clumps traveled to my brain, a stroke would almost certainly cause death.

God, I prayed, *don't let me be a vegetable, forcing my family to support me as I rot away. Just let me die if that's the case.*

Within a short time after the clinical team left my bedside, I felt as though I had been dipped into a cold bath. My teeth clapped against each other. I attempted to suck in one more remnant of air as my chest arched over the bed. That turned out to be my last voluntary movement before I lost all control of my muscles. Convulsions turned my body into something like a flopping fish out of water—my torso and limbs thrashed up and down while my head pounded with pain. The force of my heart pounding against my chest wall made me think it might burst out of my chest at any moment.

My Encounter with Jesus

Gasping for air, I felt like a floppy fish out of water. My blood cells started clumping together, causing a traffic jam throughout my veins. My heart could not keep pace with the extreme stress caused by the deadly strain of bacteria coursing through what blood flow remained in me. But then what happened next left me altogether lifeless and yet wonderfully alive.

In a nanosecond, my mind surrendered every thought to futility, and I wished I could just die. Shortly thereafter, I lost consciousness. A black void surrounded me, and I appeared to be in a space of nothingness.

That darkness engulfed my surroundings as my body floated in an airy environment. I was moving as if carried by a balloon through a haze with no awareness of what existed above except that the shades around me lightened as I ascended from pitch-black, to dark gray, to light gray, and eventually into a brilliant hue of colors illuminated by a showering light that exposed everything below and above.

In the far distance, I could see hills and figures battling with each other as I floated above them.

I had a vivid sense I was in a dimension altogether different, beyond any explanation of time or space, with one world being harsh and earthly and another ethereal and peaceful; and yet the different environments interfaced in some odd relationship that blended into an astute awareness of their interdependence. From afar, I witnessed ghastly figures lunging after towering figures bathed in the light. From above, I dared not look because of the blinding brightness.

I lingered in a serene place with a faint view of brown valleys and green rolling hills now surrounding me, and then a beam of brightness exposed everything with its shimmering illumination. My body settled upon cushy ground. Peace replaced the fear I had felt in limbo. A waft of air penetrated my body with warmth. All my fears faded.

At the time I thought, *I feel like a child settling into my favorite chair after a hard day at school, knowing that Mom is baking my favorite chocolate chip cookies.*

An assuring body leaned into me. He wrapped his arm around my torso, imparting an intensity of love beyond explanation. As I began to turn, he pressed his cheek gently into mine, then wrapped his other arm around me and hugged me tenderly.

Comfort surged through me with an assurance I had never felt before. It reminded me of times when as a child I drank warm cocoa on a cold winter day outside of Philadelphia, where I grew up, only this was a thousand times more pleasant. That first surge of warmth spread and made everything go limp.

So this is love.

I distinctly remember that one overwhelming thought, since I had never experienced love's fullness before that figure touched me.

His bright eyes tunneled into me, exposing everything dark within me. "It will be all right," he said, which confirmed what I had felt—He was Jesus.

I could literally see His figure, smell His fragrance and feel His smooth skin against my face. Everything in me spoke that truth. He was altogether familiar as a Friend and as a loving Father in one. His voice whispered.

For some strange reason, I felt as though I could not yet turn to look directly into His face, but I saw His velvety robe and felt His warmth. For most of my life, I had suffered from nasal congestion that limited my ability to taste or smell, but in that space the freshness of everything around me—flowers, pines, oranges—filled my nostrils with a fragrance more intense than I had ever experienced.

I could not speak a word. Nor did I need to speak a word, because I knew He understood me: my thoughts, my feelings and everything about me.

"Jesus," I said finally.

"Trust me, My beloved," he replied. From the corner of my eye, I could faintly see His sparkling left eye and long nose as He rested His soft face on mine. "It's not your time."

What a shame. I wanted to stay with Him and in those peaceful surroundings. The sweet perfume around me exceeded any scent of flowers I had ever smelled, and the air was fresh like after a thunderstorm. The colors around me were more intense than any I had ever beheld as I took in the green of the hills and the blue streaming waters.

Breathe . . . I could breathe.

So this is what it's like to really breathe.

For the first time in my life, I could actually breathe deeply and fill my lungs to capacity. All my life I had suffered from severe asthma and pulmonary disease and had no idea what it was like to breathe freely. Yet now each breath flowed easily and smoothly. No pain, no discomfort, no struggle remained.

Jesus and I began to walk together, and He continued holding me tightly against Him as though sensing my fear of returning. He read my thoughts, or so I understood. "Do not fear," He said. "I am with you always."

I did not feel the need to ask questions or say anything because I simply wanted to stay in this place of absolute comfort. I wanted to cry out in joy but had no tears, only a deep sense of belonging as if I was returning home after a long absence. Jesus being with me erased all concerns. I knew beyond any shadow of doubt that He would take care of everything. He was in control.

He did not need to say I love you because His very presence exuded a love I had only known faintly before this. He was pure love, indescribable by any word because His very presence embodied love. There is nothing—nothing—that even remotely describes the depth and breadth of Jesus' love, although I could see for the first time that the vastness of the universe appeared to echo the greatness of what I felt in His presence.

After some time, Jesus breathed into my face. His refreshing breath warmed me again. "You're going back," He said, "and I'm going to restore you."

I grabbed His garment like a child not wanting Him to leave home. I did not care about any surroundings; I only wanted to be with Him. I knew there was beauty around me in every sense of the word—gentle rolling hills and valleys and every part of my surroundings like some extraordinary landscape painting come to life—but all I desired was to remain close to Jesus.

And then I heard angels singing a beautiful, glorious choral song that resonated through the airwaves in perfect harmony. There must have been at least a hundred voices singing in perfect unison, and I imagined scores of angels singing the worship song. Never in all my experience had I heard such rhythmic beauty echoing within every sphere of my awareness. It soothed my soul and caused me to rejoice at the same time.

Next, Jesus hugged me and kissed me as I remembered my mother doing before I left for grade school but longed to stay home.

Then, at once, all that vanished.

I awoke on my hospital bed, my body perfectly still, and I felt the ache of someone pressing hard against my chest. Clinicians stood at my bedside, along with two visitors who were singing the very worship song I had heard with Jesus. The acrid smell of the hospital room spoiled my peace as I struggled to listen to the couple's soothing melody, because it contrasted so sharply with the pleasant fragrance I smelled with Jesus.

I was once again struggling to breathe and loathed the room's starkness. It was gray and cold, and the pungent smell of hospital disinfectants assaulted my nostrils.

To avoid my oppressive surroundings, I focused solely on the couple singing at my bedside. *Was it them I was hearing?* The song was the same. *No, there were more than two people singing that same song.* Before I heard a chorus—many voices, not just these two people.

It took some time before I understood. Angels must have joined the couple at my bedside, singing that prayerful hymn.

The prayers of those saints did indeed resonate unto the hallways of heaven. I now believe that the music was breathed from God to create some lyrical connection between heaven and earth to make my harsh transition more tolerable.

Thanks to my brush with death, I now understand 1 Corinthians 15:55 quite personally: "O death, where is your victory? O death, where is your sting?" (NLT). Transitioning from a hospital bed to the presence of the very embodiment of love tells you death has neither victory nor sting.

The Road to Recovery

After a few days, the clots in my lungs began to shrink. But even before they did, upon returning I could breathe despite the clots, as if God had opened my airways. Heavy doses of antibiotics began breaking down my systemic infection, so the chills and night sweats subsided.

Within ten days, I was able to walk the hospital floor, albeit slowly and painfully, as though dragging a wooden leg. The first time I looked outside, I looked up to the sky in hopes of seeing Jesus, feeling His embrace. I longed for it.

For several weeks after being discharged from the hospital after my NDE, I was mostly bedridden, and my recovery took months, as the valves that control blood flow in my leg had been damaged. Some valves within my vascular system had permanently collapsed, causing my blood at certain points to flow backward. My lungs were damaged, as well as other organs. I required constant anticoagulation (blood-thinning) medication, causing me to bleed and bruise.

On top of that, I experienced consistent headaches and muscle spasms that kept me up at night, as well as unexplained dizziness. I had lost about thirty pounds, so most of my clothes no longer fit. Since we did not have insurance at the time of my medical crisis, I owed over one hundred thousand dollars in medical bills. Even to this day I require routine medical attention and occasional hospital stays because of my brush with death.

I walked with a limp, wondering if I would be able to meet the demands of a job requiring constant travel. Despite it all, I began my new job. Renee traveled with me to New Jersey from our home in San Diego to help with my recovery and weekly injections of anticoagulants. Long-distance air travel frightened me since, to the best of everyone's assessments, being immobilized with no fluid intake during the flight back from my interview is what caused the deep vein thrombosis (blood clots in the calf or lower leg) that grew as time passed. Apparently, exercise may have caused some blood clots to break off and travel to my lungs. Five major clots were obstructing my airways.

That brief time I spent with Jesus represents the highlight of my life in contrast to my lowest point just before I was with Him. In a fairy tale, they could say I lived happily ever after. Of course, this life on earth is more like a roller-coaster ride. But I will never again doubt that Jesus is by my side. I know it. I can testify to you that He is real. He was not some imagined figure. He was as real as any person I have met on earth and vastly more loving.

I remained curious as to why God allowed me to suffer with a near-death experience. I asked Him to tell me why. Weeks later, He spoke in the stillness of my spirit, unlike the audible voice I heard while lying in the hospital.

This time He said, *You asked that I show Myself to you, and so I did.*

Indeed, I did want Him to "show up." Remember my desperate cry out to God when all seemed lost? I had said to Him, *This time You need to show up, God.* Indeed, I got the response for which I vehemently prayed.

And you know what? I wouldn't trade that experience for anything in the world, as strange as that may seem; because I will never question God again as to whether or not He is absolutely real and wonderfully loving. I know the answer beyond any doubt, and my hope in this book is to save you the misery of dying to meet Jesus in order to live out that reality in your own life here on earth.

Friends, be careful what you pray for. God reveals Himself in the conscience of our mind, or within our spirit, and only face-to-face in heaven. Only a departure from this life (e.g., by death or near death) ushers us to heaven. As believers, we are foreigners in this world with a purpose to accomplish in service to the King of kings. Get too comfortable in this world, and be prepared for someone or something to turn it upside down. Soon, we will return home. For now, there is work to be done in this broken world.

Now my prayers come from knowing and not from questioning. Instead of seeking answers, I seek His presence. For years after, I could not share my near-death experience with anyone except with my wife, Renee, and only a handful of friends, perhaps out of fear of being called delusional, or because it felt too personal, or maybe because Jesus wanted to keep it between just the two of us. Only recently did I feel led to share it with the world. I am by nature skeptical and formerly believed near-death experiences (NDEs) to be chemically induced, imagined, or faked. I was skeptical, that is, until I experienced my own.

Meeting Jesus face-to-face freed me to understand pain and suffering beyond my limited ability to rationalize the apparent contradiction between God's love and our struggles. After my brush with death in meeting Jesus, I understood God's love from a much different mindset. I would like to think of my transformation as me having adopted the mind of Christ more fully (see Isaiah 40:13, Romans 11:34; 1 Corinthians 2:16).

Perhaps that was my gift from heaven: the removal of all doubt that God is real, since meeting Jesus in heaven does that. Maybe sharing that revelation with you is one of the reasons

He spared my life, and because of that I now hope to impart to you the realness of God. I also hope to convey the Person of Love in a way that transcends our trivialized concept of love. That is my purpose—to reveal the reason for our faith.

Finding Joy through Sadness

Statistics tell us that your chance of having an NDE is miniscule, but the good news is that you do not need to die to know intimacy with Jesus. You do, however, need to experience the pains inflicted similarly upon each of us in this terribly fallen world. The road we will take to true joy leads through loss, sadness and pain toward a state of brokenness, purpose and empowerment, and finally an awareness of how great God's love is for you. Please do not despair that you must wait for the best to come. The journey will be well worth it. The truth is, we cannot taste of heaven's bounty without first tasting the bitterness in this world. Moreover, we cannot fully relate to God without brokenness.

One stop in your journey will be a challenge to evaluate your purpose in this life. We are "God's handiwork, created in Christ Jesus to do good works, which God prepared in advance for us to do" (Ephesians 2:10). God has a plan for you. Each of us needs to know our purpose on this earth with crystal clarity because that is the reason we were placed on this earth. Then we need to understand and practice the power of God's Holy Spirit that equips us to "fight the good fight," as the apostle Paul wrote in 1 Timothy 6:12: "Fight the good fight of the faith. Take hold of the eternal life to which you were called when you made your good confession in the presence of many witnesses." This requires power to push through the trials in life not only for ourselves but for others as well.

Toward that end, I would like to say that life proceeded smoothly after my time with Jesus in heaven. Little did I know that my greatest trials lay ahead of me. This book is about finding joy through sadness by grasping trials instead of avoiding them. Until we understand how interwoven joy and sadness are, we cannot confidently walk in faith over the long term. Eventually, the harshness of this world will wear away our belief in God's providence, and we will become hopers instead of believers—only hoping that our faith is merited.

That is not what God wants. He wants us to know Him, not to just hope for Him or imagine Him. He wants to be real to us by compelling us to get real with Him. In the process, we will discover that brokenness is truly the gateway to joy and to intimacy with God—and ultimately to paradise.

In 2 Corinthians 12:2, Paul mentioned a man who claimed to be "caught up to the third heaven." Many scholars believe Paul was talking about himself in the third person, perhaps to avoid any appearance of boastfulness as he explained in the passage. Some surmise that Paul kept quiet about this for several years and only reluctantly shared his vision after that.[2] If so, I can empathize with Paul. It took me about the same number of years to share my vision. I never wanted something so private to become so public.

I never wanted the attention to be on me. I never wanted the experience to distract from the message—that drawing near to God is paramount to a life well lived. But then my former pastor, Rich Marshall, asked me to share my NDE during a television broadcast to as many as three hundred million people, and so I did. What is more, I cried while sharing this most intimate encounter. And then Rich asked me to share about my failures with the masses.

God, I thought, *You really do work through my weaknesses, don't You?*

My vision of Jesus, which I shared with that audience and with you now, is probably similar to those visions encountered by many other followers of Christ. I am not special. Visions are common within the New Testament. Jesus' Transfiguration is described as a vision to the disciples (see Matthew 17:1–9). In Acts, Paul had a revelation of Jesus on the road to Damascus (see 22:6–11; 26:12–20), and Stephen saw a vision of Jesus at his death (see 7:55–56). John had many visions on Patmos, as recorded in the book of Revelation. The list goes on even today. I am just one of many on that list.

What matters is not whether you are on that list or not; what matters is that each one who believes in Jesus Christ as his or her Savior is written in God's "Book of Life" (Philippians 4:3; Revelation 3:5; 20:12, 15). If your name is on this list, then rest assured that you will someday meet Jesus face-to-face (see 1 Corinthians 13:12). I have only one thing to say about that encounter: Wowza!

—2—

The Sadness

Alastair Howie risked his life for a stranger—and saw
Jesus. As a workplace chaplain, he had already sacrificed
his successful banking career in response to God's calling, but
now Alastair lay on an operating room table as surgeons me-
ticulously severed the renal arteries that led from his heart to his
left kidney so the kidney could be implanted in the dying man
(whom we will call Sam) waiting in an adjoining surgical suite.

While on the operating table, Alastair saw Jesus standing
in the middle of the room. Alastair recalls: "He [Jesus] had a
smile on His face. I wanted to be with Him. Yet I knew from
His distance from me it's not yet. There is more to do." Alastair
did not just imagine Jesus; his spirit actually saw Jesus in as
much detail as we see the people around us every day.

Alastair recovered and, thanks to his donated kidney, Sam
did, too. There is more to the story, though. Just a few months
earlier, Sam's son, who had undergone a lifesaving surgery to
extract a tumor from his breast, had asked Alastair to pray
with him. So Alastair saved the lives of two generations—one

spiritually (through Christ) and one physically through a kidney transplant. My good friend Alastair models Jesus each day.

Alastair knows what it is like to be in the presence of Jesus. He saw Jesus at the most vulnerable stage of survival, as did I. We both live today still very much in Christ's presence. We do not experience mere glimpses of Jesus. Rather, we experience the reality of Jesus with each breath and every moment of our lives. Jesus is always present. It is such a shame that few of us really experience intimacy with the One who loves us most.

What about you? Does it seem that God is a part of you, or rather some distant figure? As a believer in Jesus Christ, "Don't you know that you yourselves are God's temple and that God's Spirit dwells in your midst?" (1 Corinthians 3:16). If so, why then do so many of us feel that God is only a distant figure?

I think the reason so many people feel disconnected from the God of Jesus Christ is that they envision God as too mighty, too frightening, too theoretical or too distant. We want to experience God as genuinely as we experience any one of our loved ones on earth. But "God is Spirit" (John 4:24), and so we must speak with Him through our spirit as spirit to Spirit. Our challenge in relating to God exists because there is a wall of separation between our sanctified spiritual life in Christ and our corrupted physical life in this world. Somehow that wall of separation must be torn down to allow our intimacy with God. That requires brokenness. My personal intimacy with Jesus Christ did not start with meeting Him in heaven but was found instead through brokenness.

Our Response to Suffering

God built within us two ways of responding to suffering: a neurological response and a spiritual response. The brain has built-in survival mechanisms that bridge to a spiritual awareness of what is most important, whereas our bodies respond entirely differently to suffering. Understanding both allows us to appreciate how God designed a mechanism for turning pain into gain.

To help us face grief's initial force, God constructed within our flesh and blood a mechanism whereby the hormone cortisol acts as a short-term elixir. Initially, cortisol enables us to survive emotional trauma and prevents us from falling into depression or other emotional dilemmas when we are most vulnerable. And the amygdala (sometimes called the seat of emotions within the brain) stores our painful experiences. In a crisis, such as grieving a death or battling illness, we become centered in the moment as part of God's natural design that allows us to get through it.

Hope, on the other hand, is fueled by the brain chemical serotonin.[1] The believer's spirit overrides this response to pain much like an antibody eliminates a foreign bacterium.[2] Hope in God's ability to save us opens our minds to see possibilities beyond brokenness. Psychological studies, however, reveal that humans maintain a negativity bias. Though we would like to remain positive, reminders of our failures create a kind of "doomsday mentality" or confirmation bias—a personal belief that because bad things cause a negative effect, suffering is to be avoided at all costs.

For example, during my early years I reasoned that anything painful should be avoided, so I missed several opportunities to grow. But as a young adult, I learned that pain can prove beneficial as I started pushing my limits by taking risks. As a mature Christian, I now view suffering as a means toward something much better. My circular reasoning that brokenness was to be avoided at all costs has turned into a conviction that brokenness is a means for building a stronger relationship with God.

Spiritually, brokenness produces humility in us, and God longs to produce humility in us as a means of creating a compelling need for Him. Humility allows us to recognize who God is and who we are in comparison with Him. This was the case with King David, whose moral failings loomed in his mind, reminding him again and again of his desperate need for God. Ultimately, our spirits (redeemed through Christ) thrive through brokenness.

As Christ's followers, we can view suffering through a perspective of God's grace that helps renew our minds and restore our faith. For instance, before facing my own mortality I desperately feared death. It took seeing death as a pathway toward my eternity through Christ to cause my mind to interpret brokenness as a means toward absolute joy in heaven. Now I no longer fear death because I perceive it as a gateway to a far better life.

Understanding God's Character

As believers, brokenness yields our bodies to our sanctified spirits when we can view hope in place of despair, and when God's reality supersedes our reality in this world. Genuinely understanding God's personhood begins to break away negative preconceptions that serve to divide the children of God from their loving Father. Before my brokenness, I did not truly understand the character of God.

I learned in the darkest places that compassion and understanding represent two of God's more significant traits. More than twenty verses reference the compassion of Jesus Christ, of which one of the most recognizable is His statement in Matthew 11:28: "Come to Me, all who are weary and heavy-laden, and I will give you rest" (NASB).

Jesus experienced all the sufferings and pains of the human condition without abandoning His uncorrupted self and while taking on the burdens of others. He understands our struggles like none other because, as the Son of God, He "looks at the heart" (1 Samuel 16:7), knowing us even better than we know ourselves. Jesus also forgave even the most reviled in society, as in the story of the woman caught in adultery (see John 8:3–11).

Jesus' compassionate grace was a trait that overwhelmed me to tears when I met Him.

Understanding Jesus' peaceful, compassionate, empathetic, and merciful character is imperative to fathoming the most troubling question: Why does God allow suffering to happen to His beloved children? The answer lies squarely with how we are being conformed to the character of Jesus Christ through brokenness. Trials peel away the coarsening effect of this world so that we can experience God more fully. In so doing, we become more like Christ. Although the ultimate outcome is joy, the process can be painful, as was the case with Jesus Christ's journey on earth. Indeed, all the people we see or meet are going through some struggle unbeknownst to us, even if they say everything is "fine."

When hope in Christ replaces stored feelings of suffering, thanks to the brain's plasticity, our minds are renewed with joy in place of sadness. For instance, I only faintly recall my suffering in the hospital, but my memories of God's love remain as fresh as the scent of flowering buds in springtime. The memory is kind. My brain's experiences found an alternative pathway through my born-again spirit that created a renewed hope and wonder about God's reality in my life.

According to Galatians 5:17, our minds and bodily cravings are continually battling the Spirit, and this keeps us from doing the things we want to do. This explains why we need to be broken of destructive habits to receive the fullness God desires for us. Eventually, though, intimacy with God will replace the grief that results from our physical loss, and this will usher in a fresh relationship with the Holy Spirit.

Jonathan's Story

The story of Jonathan demonstrates the transformational effect of brokenness under the watchful eye of a loving father. In this case, I was Jonathan's foster father. He came to me as a "last resort," the caseworker said. He had hopped from foster home to foster home, in each one committing some act of rebellion until at last the only placement left for him was a detention center for wayward teens. He was not quite thirteen, and shortly after we met, he threw a punch at me when I insisted he should not go out to join his "friends," who were drug dealers according to the caseworker. That was the first of many attempts Jonathan made to push me away. He kept me on my knees before God. Through many trials, Jonathan began to realize that I was truly committed to him and that I genuinely loved him as a father.

Jonathan came from a cultic family. His biological father wanted nothing to do with him. His mother then married a man who resorted to a cruel form of physical punishment whenever the boy rebelled. Jonathan also endured "shunning" (sitting in the center of the room without essentials and with absolutely no communication) and verbal abuse (he was told he would "amount to nothing"). And so, this impressionable boy with a genius IQ lowered his esteem to match the demeaning accusations of his family, and that is how he ended up in foster care after committing a series of misdeeds.

Though I was fully prepared to adopt Jonathan, the caseworker decided to place him back with his abusive family. I had already adopted Jonathan in my heart. Day and night, I cried to God, asking Him to protect this boy. God replied to me within the stillness of my heart, assuring me that Jonathan was within His loving care. Years passed. I visited Jonathan at a detention center for teen offenders, seeing him as often as possible. As an adult, he joined the U.S. Navy, worked as a paramedic and tried his best to escape the cycle of abuse that many abused children repeat as adults.

Given the distant and mostly harsh environments in which he lived, I could only remotely be a father to Jonathan. But I did pray for him each day. I committed him into God's hands.

Both God and I were invisible fathers for Jonathan. Jonathan oftentimes felt abandoned. Little did he know that I frequently checked on his safety without his knowledge while God silently watched over him.

Jonathan's case brings to mind my favorite allegorical poem, "Footprints in the Sand," which tells the story of Jesus' carrying us during our most difficult times even while we cannot see Him. This poem tells of a troubled man walking along in the sand with the Lord. The man says: "I noticed that during the saddest and most troublesome times of my life, there was only one set of footprints." God whispered, "My precious child, I love you and will never leave you never, ever, during your trials and tests. When you saw only one set of footprints, it was then that I carried you."[3]

Jonathan's sufferings and my inability to intervene on his behalf racked my soul. Still, I knew that my Father watched over Jonathan's comings and goings (see Psalm 121:8). God would shield him (see Deuteronomy 32:10) and teach him in the way he should go, counseling this vulnerable young man with His "loving eye" on him (Psalm 32:8).

And that is exactly what God did. Today Jonathan is a thriving physician who graduated with both a master of business administration (M.B.A.) and a doctor of medicine (M.D.). He manages hospital programs throughout the United States, is married to a wonderful woman and has helped thousands of diseased and downtrodden people throughout the world, often traveling to Asia to provide medical and surgical care to populations too poor to receive even basic healthcare. Jonathan is doing what he loves to do, and I am very proud of him.

My point in sharing Jonathan's story is that we, like him, have been abused by this world and its effects, felt abandoned at times and are very much loved by a Father who remains committed to staying by our side. Even though we may feel distant from God, He is always present in our lives. It took countless trials, suffering and brokenness to make Jonathan the healer of those who suffer. His purpose and joy are not an exception to his trials but the result of them.

Finding Joy in Trials

To find joy, you and I must first endure the inevitable sadness that precedes it. This is an irony of the fallen human condition, even though we, like Jonathan, are always loved by the Father. There is a symbiotic relationship between suffering and joy somewhat analogous to the pain of surgery to repair a damaged organ or bone that eventually results in a new lease on life. Suffering and joy seem like opposites, yet in God's Kingdom they are intertwined in this life. All of God's saints faced trials of various sorts. One cannot experience lasting joy without the sadness in this world. There is no sadness in heaven, yet in this world sadness is the pathway toward genuine relationship with God and others.

In this world we live as orphaned believers predestined with the purpose of being conformed to the image of Jesus Christ (see Romans 8:29). And that requires being molded like the proverbial potter's clay. This world taints us and tends to conform us to its image, not to Christ's. If you have ever lost your temper after being cut off on the freeway or been tempted to do something you know is wrong, then you know what I mean. We often succumb to the world's pressures and temptations. So instead of being conformed to this world, we must be remolded in conformity with Christ. And that requires brokenness.

One verse speaks directly about this conundrum: "Consider it pure joy, my brothers and sisters, whenever you face trials of many kinds" (James 1:2). Trials tend to break us. They sometimes humiliate us. That brokenness is not a choice; it is a gift. After experiencing the comforting embrace of Jesus, I came to know that only being in His presence elicits absolute joy, but it follows brokenness.

God's Word says that we should find joy in trials. Paul even wrote in Philippians 2:18 that we should rejoice at the prospect of death. None of us wants to die. Yet death precedes life with Christ. That does not make sense in the natural mind, but in the language of the heart, we yearn for a loftier place than our present circumstances, even if it must be born from the ashes. God inverts human wisdom (see 1 Corinthians 1:18–19, 27–30). He subverts our mindfulness with the mind of Christ (see Philippians 2:5–8), forcing us to believe in the unbelievable beyond what the human mind can comprehend.

Facing the "Eeyore Complex"

By reasoning, I presumed that my faith could overcome any trials after meeting Jesus. I had touched Him, talked with Him. Yet so did the disciples who rejected Christ. Instead of enjoying a life of peace after Christ rose from the dead after being crucified on the cross, each one of them suffered persecution.

Traditional accounts say that Andrew was crucified in Greece. Bartholomew, missionary to India, was crucified upside down in Albania. James son of Alphaeus was stoned in Jerusalem. James son of Zebedee was beheaded. John was banished to Patmos to die in exile. Peter was crucified upside down in Rome, as was Philip in Turkey. Thomas was speared to death in Afghanistan. The rest died of old age, even though all suffered persecution.[4] How did these martyrs endure this excruciating suffering after casually rejecting Jesus before He went to the cross? Because the walk of Christ breaks the need to cling to this broken world so we can cling to God.

So I should not have been surprised that my trials would continue after recovering from my near-death experience. Indeed, my greatest suffering lay ahead of me. I call it my sadness. Through that sadness, I realized the love of God in a profound measure equal to the embrace of Love Himself.

Before the sadness, I believed that Christians should be cheery and joyful since joy is one of the spiritual fruits listed in Galatians 5:22–23. I really did feel that way. Whenever I met an effervescent and happy Christian, it convicted me—I should be the same, right? But mild depression played within my mind for much of my life. There would be nights when I would stare at the ceiling into a dark hole from which I could not escape. Darkness often spread within my mind whenever I felt rejected. Sometimes my depression played out as a sense of pessimism, creating a false belief in the inevitability of failure and disappointment.

We jokingly refer to it as the "Eeyore Complex" in our family, named after the gloomy, depressed and generally pessimistic donkey from the Winnie the Pooh books by A. A. Milne. In all seriousness, depression is a mental disorder. When he was a child, my son, Ryan, favored Eeyore more than any other storybook character, which portended my long-held fear that he would inherit the illness. Today Ryan is a strong man of integrity who sets low expectations for people and situations in order to remain pleasantly surprised when those expectations are exceeded. This is a common coping mechanism to offset the clinical sadness of depression. I feel his pain—and I lament passing the sadness on to him, even though I admire his courage and strength.

It was not just my depression that caused the sadness. The sadness came from a far worse situation than anything imaginable. Regrettably, each member of my family suffers from some form of mental illness.

Annie's Sadness

My daughter, Annie, was born with rosy cheeks and a Cheshire grin that bloomed on her face for most of her young childhood. On sunny days, she frolicked around the playground wearing her signature lime-colored bonnet and frilly outfits, jiggling her head from side to side as she played in the sand and giggled with abandonment. Joy accompanied her day and night until the sadness happened.

Annie began experiencing ministrokes in fifth grade, caused by a hemiplegic migraine disorder. She lost all memory of her childhood through a series of debilitating strokes. Her personality changed. She suffered with anxiety. Night terrors became a normal occurrence.

Those terror screams still haunt me today.

When Annie's body broke out in psoriasis, kids teased her at school. Teachers chastised her for being belligerent. Did I rejoice amid trials as James 1:2 calls us to do? No, I did not rejoice. Seeing my daughter come home from school in tears caused a flood of anger, frustration and confusion as to why God would permit such faithful Christians to endure this kind of pain. Worse than any personal pain is witnessing the pain of a loved one, especially one's child. I could cope with my own suffering, but not my child's.

I kept asking God, *Why Annie?*

As she entered the challenging adolescent years, Annie's once-sunny disposition turned to violent mood swings. She self-medicated with cocaine, methamphetamine (meth) and other illicit drugs. These drugs caused Annie's volatile and often violent behaviors.

One night left me almost hopeless. I received a call from the police station telling me to come get my daughter. When I arrived at the station, one of the police officers told me that Annie's boyfriend was being charged. His fellow gang members got into a scuffle, and Annie's boyfriend threatened another gang member. My daughter happened to be along for the ride.

"Did you know your daughter's been using meth?" the officer asked.

"No," I replied.

"She confessed it," he said.

Then another officer brought Annie out into the waiting room so I could take her home. She was not being charged.

During the ride home, I suggested getting a restraining order against the boyfriend since his gang affiliation had been confirmed. Annie threatened to jump out of the car in response to my threat. We made it home, and Annie stormed around the house, crashing doors, shouting profanities, and kicking a hole through the wall. It was the drugs, I surmised, trying to explain her violent behavior. I attempted to physically restrain Annie from causing any further damage. But she kicked and screamed, her strength being far greater than her thin five-foot-two frame would seemingly allow.

I picked up the landline phone to call for help. Annie screamed at me to put down the phone. She threatened to kill herself. When I continued dialing 911 out of fear for Annie and me, she yanked the phone line out of the outlet and ran out of my home office. I completed the call from my cell phone and began searching each of the fifteen rooms in our house. Not finding her upstairs, I ran downstairs and finally found her in the kitchen, standing in the corner with tears streaming down her face and a ten-inch kitchen knife pressed against her chest.

"Don't come any closer or I'll kill myself," she said.

"Don't do this," I pleaded. 'We'll work this out. It will be okay. Just put the knife down." Silently, I implored God to rescue my daughter.

Annie's face cringed, her lips pursed and her eyes cut through me with a ghoulish stare. She pointed the knife toward me. "Or . . . maybe I'll just kill you!" She stepped toward me as I backed up, planning to snatch the knife, but then she broke into a run toward me.

Hearing a knock, I turned and ran toward the front door. As I opened the door, Annie stood about six feet behind me with the knife in her clutch.

The police officer at the door asked, "What's going on?"

As soon as she saw the officer, Annie ran upstairs to hide.

The officer asked me to go outside with him so I could explain the situation. I implored him not to hurt Annie, to not use force. The six to eight police officers now assembled assured me they would not use their guns.

Annie knew I had a shotgun in a locked safe, but I had hidden the key, so there was no chance of her accessing the shotgun. My fear was that she would stab herself. I was praying like crazy, asking God to protect Annie.

After about ten minutes, Annie shouted from her upstairs bathroom window, promising she would not hurt herself or anyone else. She stated she had left the knife in the kitchen sink.

That is when we went inside the house. Annie came downstairs, crying hysterically. The police took her to the hospital, and I followed. Annie was treated there for a few days and thereafter spent time at a dual-diagnosis treatment center in L.A.

The combination of drugs and Annie's mental illness caused this crisis, coupled with, I believe, a demonic attack. That was the night from hell. And my wife agrees with me that for years our struggles with Annie were like a living hell. The struggles in coping with the effects of drugs and Annie's anxiety disorder continued in and out of treatment centers, more holes in the walls, ineffective therapies, etc.

Indeed, it seemed as if the devil kept his thumb on my daughter from adolescence. I will never forget my precious daughter saying to me, "Daddy, I don't want to be this way." I wept—still do at times.

Our son, Ryan, experienced sleepless nights, thinking his little sister might one day fulfill her pledge to kill him. During high school, he faced the sadness as acne spread rapidly across his face. He played video games with few social contacts despite our encouragements to "get out and be with others." Trapped in a dark malaise, he wore a hoodie to cover his otherwise handsome face because of the facial scarring.

Though Annie loved Ryan, the terrible irony of her disorder is that those closest to the emotionally afflicted face the brunt of the afflicted person's ire. My wife, Renee, who suffered from chronic anxiety, likened our angst to post-traumatic stress disorder (PTSD). Renee, Ryan and I felt as if we were walking on eggshells constantly, not wanting to provoke an outburst. Annie, for her part, felt increasingly more isolated.

During her teen years, Annie developed Tourette syndrome, causing her to blurt out loud noises. Lack of impulse control, aggression, and anger outbursts are common effects of Tourette syndrome. Imagine the embarrassment this caused our beautiful young teen around her peers. Annie's tortured state of mind also caused uncontrollable screaming throughout a seven-hour flight to Europe. All we could do was give her a pillow to buffer the screams.

My dear readers, that explains the toll of mental illness and oppression. It robs family members of their joy. For those of you who have suffered likewise, I say, "God bless you." I understand your pain. I now know "the LORD is my strength and shield" (Psalm 28:7), and the "joy of the LORD is [my] strength," as Nehemiah 8:10 declares. Many days and nights, we prayed. And many times, God's presence soothed our trepidation of not knowing when the next crisis might happen. But it was a hellacious existence.

My time with Jesus (the NDE) drew me to sometimes ask God if He could just make the experience "permanent." My NDE with Jesus always gave me strength, but the overwhelming love Jesus had for me during that time consistently reminded me that my purpose had yet to be fulfilled in this world. I always knew that Jesus would turn everything around for good, which has been born out time and time again. God is *good*.

More Trials on the Horizon

The prospect of abandoning Renee and my family again because of another medical emergency loomed over my head like a wrecking ball. I worried that blood clots would form in my lungs from another long flight or from being sedentary for too long. Sure enough, while exercising one day I felt the same heaviness in my calf. This time I made an appointment to have it checked. An ultrasound confirmed another clot. I was immediately placed on blood thinners and went home. The clot stopped traveling toward my lungs. Instead of a free fall toward death, this time God provided me with a parachute to prevent another crash. I could still provide for my family. *Thank you, Jesus*, I prayed. It seemed as if a crisis was always waiting around the corner for us.

That next crisis happened one Christmas night when Annie, who was then eighteen years old, attended a party with friends. A young man drugged Annie and her friend, then sexually assaulted them. We turned off the Christmas tree lights that night, both figuratively and literally. The scourge of that violation incited my rage. At one point at the gym, I thought that I saw that rapist's backside. At full speed, I raced over to the man, causing him to spin around and freeze. He was not the rapist, but this shocking response revealed my rageful potential for violence.

Many would say that God allowed my daughter to be raped. God knew the horrendous damage inflicted upon Annie. Why did He not stop it? Why did He not strike down the rapist before it happened? These questions only serve to hide the truth of why bad things happen. The truth is that people who commit atrocities always defy God. They are degenerate—and those of us who love God are daily exposed to the effects of this sinful world.

If we ask why God does not save us from violations, then we should also ask this question: Why did Jesus not save Himself from being tortured and hung on the cross? The reason is that God always provides redemption through others' cruelties. We desire God's unfailing love, but we must endure the failures of others in this sullied world.

Sometimes God allows suffering for a redemptive reason, as when God removed His protective covering in allowing Satan to torment Job for a season. From our limited perspective, we might consider God cruel for allowing Job to lose almost everything. Whenever God permits us to lose something, however, He always gives another blessing of greater "heavenly value" in return. Though in the end God rewarded Job with twofold more than he had previously, the heavenly value returned for Job's suffering was his testimony of perseverance and of God's faithfulness through pain from which countless others have benefitted—people like you and me. The story of Job speaks to the heavenly treasures God promises to all who suffer in Christ. As long as we stay truthful with ourselves and with God, we will reap our heavenly reward as a gift of redemption.

Consider what Proverbs 19:22 says: "What a person desires is unfailing love; better to be poor than a liar." This proverb explains how we tend to cover up our doubts, our real feelings, and then bury the parts of ourselves that are injured, thus causing us sometimes to blame God. The proverb writer is merely stating that a person is better off poor than resorting to a dishonest cover-up or deflecting one's anger toward God.

Let's get real with God and each other by sharing our hurts and trusting God to redeem us from sinfulness. The only path toward wholeness is realness. I cry to this day that Annie suffered at the hands of someone I could not stop, but I do not blame God. Today, Annie helps heal those similarly affected because she knows their anguish.

Should I have shouted with joy at the time of this trial? Of course not. Let's get real, folks. It is hard to shout, "Praise the

Lord, hallelujah" when the foot of catastrophe wedges itself between the people you love and the truth you desperately try to hold on to. Imagine your child saying, "You're an f-ing freak," "You're a failure as a father," "F--- you," and countless other vile accusations. These paled against the suffering I knew existed within my daughter's fragile heart. You might say Annie's abuses deserved some form of discipline, and I agree.

But given my current understanding of the scourge of drugs and mental illness, I know that the need for discipline must be tempered by an element of grace. Maybe you have heard or believed that God deserves to render judgment on a world that by and large has forsaken Him. But then again, the grace of God sometimes passes over our transgressions. God is a God of judgment, but He is also a God of grace. Moreover, although this fallen world brings much sadness, God allows its effects to be used for His purpose and the purpose for which He created us.

When the sadness came upon Annie and the rest of our family through mental illness, drugs and rape, it clouded over our joy. Over several years, I spent thousands of dollars in out-of-pocket medical expenses on psychiatric clinics and hospitals, trying to fix our family while waiting for some miracle. One highly rated treatment center in the Chicago area cost us over a thousand dollars a day. The constant stress imperiled my marriage as Renee and I vented our frustrations on each other.

And then our imagined nightmare became reality. Annie attempted suicide after swallowing several pills one evening after a breakup with her boyfriend. I sat in the emergency room with Annie as she flatlined.

"Is she with you?" I asked Jesus, who only months before spoke to me from my hospital bed.

The charcoal Annie had taken to absorb the poisons dripped from her mouth. She was pale, lifeless.

"God, save her!" I shouted out loud. "Take me—not her!"

Then a quiet voice spoke within me: *Trust me.*

It was always that same promise—*trust me.* That familiar voice spoke to me again in the depths of my heart. So I let go and let God do His work.

The resuscitation team arrived in our cramped room with their equipment to revive Annie. The first attempt failed.

I spoke silently to God. *I'm not done learning from her.*

Annie was teaching me something transformative. I knew it in my spirit. I needed Annie to help me break through my hard-headedness and judgmental attitude in order to gain a better perspective. I knew Annie was the key to finding joy through the sadness. Indeed, she was teaching me about the Father's love.

What followed was altogether familiar. A peace surpassing the crisis settled in my soul. My spirit spoke: *You've got this, Lord.* The minutes shrank to seconds as I entered that holy place beyond my wants, the Father's will. Whatever might happen now, in the end it would be good either on earth or in heaven.

The whole time, I continued to "pray in the Spirit." The Bible mentions praying in the Spirit as a most powerful form of prayer (see Ephesians 6:18; 1 Corinthians 14:15; Jude 20). Simply put, it means praying with the leading of God's Spirit. That is how I prayed—asking God to direct my prayers and then trusting Him to do so.

Annie's chest puffed out with a deep breath. Her eyes opened. She looked around as if searching for someone.

"Jesus is here," I said. "You just can't see Him."

Annie's heart rhythm on the monitor returned to normal. She survived. This time, the authors of death in the nether world lost. This attack, perpetrated by the rulers and authorities in the unseen realm and the evil spirits in heavenly places described in Ephesians 6:12, had failed. These dark powers had succumbed to God's dominion. I now recall the battles I once saw after my encounter with death—the same warfare being played out in Annie's near-death experience.

Though Annie fully recovered, I wondered if she might someday fulfill her pledge to kill herself. That possibility replayed in my mind for a long time, especially when drama would erupt over something as inane as a nasty Facebook post that triggered an outburst or when Annie suffered a serious blow such as a car accident that ruptured her spleen. What is worse, Annie denied that God existed because as she either implied or said, Why would God allow her to suffer like this?

People would try to coach Renee and me on how to help our daughter. Some people encouraged us to use "tough love," while others preached "grace." Secretly, we felt judged. I resigned from a church board believing that I had failed as a father. God never shames us when our children or loved ones rebel, but people sometimes do. As a young adult, I absorbed advice from James Dobson, founder of Focus on the Family, which counseled parents on how to develop a strong family. That idyllic picture of a strong family only served to convict me as I questioned whether or not I had failed my family, both as a father and a husband.

I learned through God's example that my overriding responsibility was to love Annie. When the prodigal son returned to his father, the story in Luke went this way: "So he got up and went to his father. But while he was still a long way off, his father saw him and was filled with compassion for him; he ran to his son, threw his arms around him and kissed him" (15:20). The father's love was unconditional. He did not chastise his wayward son; he just loved him. This represents how God the Father responds to our brokenness through failures.

God's Response to Brokenness

It would be wonderful if we could adopt God's way of responding to brokenness, right? Our tendency is to fix what is broken, not to simply love it. This causes anxiety. Suffering from blood clots choking me to death or the loss of a job and income all seemed like a cakewalk compared to the mental anguish of watching a child suffer and a family being torn apart. Prayer at times seemed only to assuage our hardship.

Through much of this season of trials, joy seemed elusive. Unbeknownst to me, God was revealing a profound heart lesson while constructing a bridge to joy. God's bridge-building materials consisted of stepping-stones to a new dwelling place that would free each of us to experience God's joy in place of the thoughts that imprisoned us with fear. That dwelling place is within God's presence born out of brokenness.

I did not have to die to be with Jesus. Rather, I needed to live life through brokenness to realize God's abundance. The irony of God's choosing someone struggling with depression to reveal the joy in sadness through this book did not escape me.

Why don't you pick one of those perky Christians to let people know how to achieve joy through brokenness? I asked God.

His response was something like this: *I chose you, My beloved, because you know the depth of My joy apart from this world.*

Maybe God could expose His brilliance most vividly through the striking contrast of the gray-colored lenses of my mind.

Stripped bare of any rationale for suffering or a solution for it, the human mind gives way to the spirit mind of Christ. Our thinking becomes something like this: *This is beyond me, God, so it's entirely up to You now.* Suffering invades the depths of our soul, often making us feel abandoned, alone, ashamed. And yet it is out of that abyss, that void, that God alone can find us humbled and yielding, stripped raw of all pretenses. Through the sadness, we discover His lasting joy and not just some temporary state of happiness.

The truth Paul revealed in 2 Corinthians 12:9–11 explains the key to finding joy through giving up all hope to God:

> But he said to me, "My grace is sufficient for you, for my power is made perfect in weakness." Therefore, I will boast all the more gladly about my weaknesses, so that Christ's power may rest on me. That is why, for Christ's sake, I delight in weaknesses, in insults, in hardships, in persecutions, in difficulties. For when I am weak, then I am strong.

Our weakness lies at the heart of deep relationship with Christ. When I could not do anything to save Annie from death, my only recourse was to trust in God. I gave up. I was too weak to do anything. That is the position we must be in for God to take over—surrender. It allows His Spirit to take over from our body and mind, yielding them to our born-again spirit through Christ. It allows God's Spirit to speak uninterrupted with our spirit. God takes control.

The sadness each of us experiences happens for a reason. It forces us to give up and live up to God. Brought to the utmost level of despair, we surrender the keys to our life unto the God of all creation, and then He takes control. And once God takes control, He can relate to us in power and intimacy. That leads to a lasting joy through the "renewing of your mind" (Romans 12:2) in concert with our reborn spirit that relates most intimately with God.

Our natural body and that inner self (the "flesh"), which is alienated from God, oppose God's Holy Spirit, who resides in each believer (Galatians 5:17). The two are constantly fighting with each other, oftentimes preventing us from carrying out our best intentions. This is why our minds must be continually cleansed from the negative effects of this world. Romans 12:2 says it this way: "Do not conform to the pattern of this world, but be transformed by the renewing of your mind. Then you will be able to test and approve what God's will is—his good, pleasing and perfect will."

How do we renew our minds? By spending time with God, reading the Bible and praying. Yes, of course, but the conundrum in our walk with Christ is that only by going through the inevitable disappointments and suffering in this fallen world can God strip us of a fixed mindset to accept His reality over our reality.

A fixed mindset tells us that only limited possibilities exist within the context of our determination or comprehension. For example, we cannot reason how the universe was created in six days; the fixed human mindset reasons, therefore, some explanation like the Big Bang theory, which is nevertheless equally implausible because the human mind, not God, determined it. A God mindset says that all things are possible through Christ (see Philippians 4:13). His words and promises supersede our mind's need to rationalize them.

In the presence of God, all suffering is stripped away and replaced with comfort and joy. Joy is a condition of the heart, not an emotion like happiness. Joy is created through a relationship with God's Holy Spirit that enters us, makes us feel good and opens our spiritual eyes to see the blessings of Christ in all things.

That is how I battled the ravages of the mental illnesses that affected my loved ones and me. This is how I have reached an intimacy with Jesus equal to my encounter with Him in heaven. Most people love to hear about my near-death experience with Jesus. I know we all need assurances now and then that Jesus is indeed real and alive, and who better to testify of Jesus than those who claim to have met Him face-to-face?

I am here to tell you, however, that you can reach absolute intimacy with Christ without dying physically. You simply need to embrace your sadness as a vehicle to strip away the flesh, and make yourself empty, so you can be filled with God's presence. Stop trying to fight the sadness, and instead use it as a means toward a joyful end. Reframe that failure or fracture as an opportunity to see God turn ashes into beauty (Isaiah 61:3).

A Happy Ending for Annie

Today, I am pleased to share that Annie has taught me more about God's love than anyone else. As her parent, I know in my small way how God loves even His most rebellious children and why He loves me despite all my flaws. In God's eyes, I am no different from Annie. I have rebelled, I have cursed God and I have immersed myself in the things of this world. Through Annie, I have learned the power of forgiveness and grace.

I know how drugs and mental illness rob people of reason, thus preventing them from doing what is good; and this made me less judgmental and more understanding of others. In that same way, I know the grace of God, which sees the world's stain upon our hearts that prevents us from being good. I feel as if I have been trained in "the boot camp of suffering" to be better prepared to battle with the negative influences of this world. As a result, I can love more fully.

I thank God that He brought me trials, which is not to say that I would not prefer that Annie had been saved from her trials or that I did not suffer from depression. I thank God, rather, for turning our experiences for good such that we can love more like Jesus does. Moreover, I am delighted to announce Annie now testifies of Jesus as her Lord and Savior. If we need help, Annie is the first one to volunteer it with no questions asked. She now faces each trial with the belief that "this too shall pass." She understands the depth of true love. Annie is our family's greatest evangelist because she knows God's grace through suffering, making her sensitive to the poor and downtrodden. Our little girl, whom we once referred to as having "a heart of gold," has been refined through the furnace of suffering to produce a genuine heart of gold in Christ.

One late night after a street fair in San Diego, my wife and I looked around and could not find Annie. After a short search, we saw her sitting on a corner, speaking with a transgender teenager with torn leggings tightly hugging his legs, mascara dripping down his face from a steady stream of tears. No one cared for that homeless youth that day, except Annie.

Because of Annie's own brokenness, she had compassion for this broken teen who felt abandoned. Annie showed an otherwise unloved human being God's true love. Such is the empathy that connects those healed from brokenness with the forgotten broken people of this world. That is the fruit of Annie's brokenness. That is love.

— 3 —

Walking with a Limp

In this age of grace (after His sacrificial death on the cross), each believer can realize amazing intimacy with God through Christ. After Jesus ascended into heaven, God sent the Holy Spirit to indwell those who believe in Him (see John 16:7), so Jesus can mediate between the Father and His children (see 1 Timothy 2:5). In Matthew, Jesus told His disciples, "I will give you the keys of the kingdom of heaven" (16:19), "with God all things are possible" (19:26), and that "all authority in heaven and on earth" had been given to Him (28:18).

Jesus can do anything. If He wants to shift the elements of time and space, He can do that. Through a bizarre incident that took place in Southern California decades ago, I experienced firsthand how Jesus can do anything. In my case, He even had the power to alter reality.

After showing the late-night shift of nurses and physicians at a hospital in Los Angeles how to use a new diagnostic monitor, I began traveling up the highway to a hospital in Santa Barbara to in-service the staff there. Having had no sleep, I began to doze off while driving, then was shocked into noticing a car's headlights beaming directly into my face. Both of us must have been speeding above the sixty-five-miles-per-hour speed limit and had no time to avoid each other on a two-lane road within a split second of a head-on collision.

That happened more than thirty years ago, and to this day, I cannot explain what happened next. At the instant of the would-be accident, my next recollection was seeing the taillights of that car in my rearview mirror. At no time had I fallen asleep given my alarm in preparing for a crash, and yet for some unexplained reason, there was a juxtaposition of physics and space as God seemed to leap one car over another in some weird "time warp."

Accepting this apparent miracle as the work of God represents a God mindset. I cannot explain it, but I believe it because I know Jesus, and He can do anything. We also call this faith. Remaining in a constant state of faith to accept God's reality as our reality requires a renewal of the mind. Renewing, or changing, that mindset requires brokenness. It so happens that those closest to God have been broken. And God is intimate with the brokenhearted. They know their Father's voice.

We ~~Dis~~Proved Christianity

"The LORD is close to the brokenhearted and saves those who are crushed in spirit. The righteous person may have many troubles, but the LORD delivers him from them all" (Psalm 34:18–19). If you want to get close to God, you must be broken because, as David wrote, "a broken and contrite heart you, God, will not despise" (51:17). The fundamental need of believers in Jesus Christ is a recognition of our damaged and flawed nature so that our failings may bring us to a point of desiring God all the more.

That was certainly not me as a young man. Ever heard the story of Paul's conversion after meeting Jesus on the road to

Damascus? During his days of stoning Christians to death, they called him Saul. You would be hard-pressed to find anyone who hated Christians more than Saul.

As a young man, I could identify with Saul. In my late teens and early twenties, I am quite sure that if there had been some legal and socially acceptable way of silencing Christians, I would have been the first in line to do so. An ardent agnostic during my college years, I championed the movement to get the Christian Club banned from Northwestern University's campus. Outwardly, I contested that religion should be confined to private meetings, not public forums on university grounds. Inwardly, I reasoned, *All Christians are just hypocrites*. Indeed, several so-called Christians proselytized me while sleeping with their girlfriends or boyfriends and using the same foul language and practicing the same vile habits as the rest of us.

Then I read a book by Joni Eareckson Tada. For those not familiar with Joni, she became a quadriplegic after a diving accident in 1967 while just seventeen (she was born in 1949 and has been paralyzed for well over fifty years). Since the accident, she has gone on to author over fifty books, preach the Good News of Jesus Christ to hundreds of thousands in packed-out stadiums and churches, host a daily radio program for almost forty years, and supply people around the world with wheelchairs. A world-renowned artist, she creates masterpieces with her mouth and a brush or pen.

After listening to her cheery and upbeat messages on the radio, I concluded, *If this lady can accept Jesus after the hell she has gone through, then she must be for real*. Thus, at 23, I called out to an unknown God, *If You're real, I have to know You as real as the people who are my friends and family*. I would not be satisfied by a book, the Bible or some imagined feeling. But nothing really happened after that "prayer."

A short while later, I asked a few of my techy friends to help test all the major religions. At least, I thought, an earnest research of religions might expose the truth. Secretly, I wanted to disprove all religions. One brilliant computer science major plugged data into a computer the size of an entire building at Northwestern University. We used data points such as prophecies and proclamations in the Bible, the Torah, the Koran and various Hindu as well as Buddhist writings to assess which proved true and which proved false. We challenged the validity of each religious foundation by corroborating stories or books to determine contradictions.

Our brainiacs measured the time lapse between the completion of ancient documents and when the oldest available copies were made and the number of copies made, matching them up with each other. Take for example Homer's *Iliad*, the earliest existing manuscript of which was written almost 1,500 years after the earliest copy from the eighth century BC. By contrast, the research showed that the Bible has a lapse of a hundred years and a consistency between all documents of over 95 percent—meaning it was the most well-validated ancient writing on record and the oldest ancient literary work at twenty thousand years. Written by more than forty authors, the Bible covers hundreds of subjects, and of the experts we researched, not one could find a single contradiction.

Remember that I was an agnostic at that time, as were all the researchers and analyzers helping me. The statistical probability of the Bible being accurate proved to be 1.26 million to 1. All the other religions were falsified because of conflicting historical accounts or uncorroborated statements from their founders, who were usually flawed human beings claiming personal revelations.

From our objective analysis, only one religion proved exclusive. We found that you could be a Buddhist and accept Jesus as truthful. You could be a Muslim and believe in Jesus as a prophet or truth teller. You could be a Hindu or New Ager and accept the "universality" of truth. You could not, however, be a

Christian and believe in the truth of any other religion, because Jesus Himself made this exclusive proclamation: "I am the way and the truth and the life. No one comes to the Father except through me" (John 14:6). That factor—a consistently relatable God—differentiates Christianity from all other religions.

Unlike other religions based on a single founder or a fusion of ancient beliefs, Christianity formed through the account of multigenerational authors who corroborate a consistent lineage leading to Jesus Christ. Christianity resulted from thousands of linked stories from multiple sources spanning some 3,400 years and all pointing to the God of the Bible. This unequaled storyline of God pointed exclusively to Jesus Christ as the only way to establish a relationship with God. My earnest research of religions led me to only one conclusion: either accept Jesus Christ as the only way to God or refuse to accept God at all.

To a devoted skeptic such as myself, this proof only confirmed the *probability* of Christianity. Until I met Jesus *personally*, all the proof in the world would be just theory. And that was fine with God, because head knowledge without the heart knowledge of Jesus Christ amounts to just a cursory and fragile understanding of Him. Instead, God desires intimacy (see John 14:21; James 4:8). As with any relationship, this requires trusting in God's promises. A biblical knowledge must grow our trust in God (see Proverbs 3:5); otherwise, our pride grows.

God Saved a Scoundrel

After graduating from college, I continued to place my faith in the god of success. But after I landed my first job (with Procter & Gamble), I witnessed my first death-defying miracle. I was driving on a Cincinnati freeway when a station wagon leaped over a barricade and plowed head-on into my car, causing my car to spin. The force thrust my head into the windshield since, foolish me, I had not buckled my seat belt. Next, my little compact vehicle wrapped its chassis around a light pole before tumbling over an embankment into a ditch.

I emerged from my mangled car with a broken windshield and barely a scratch. Fortunately, the person who fell asleep at the wheel, causing her car to jump the barricade and hit me, survived.

Nothing but scrap metal survived of my former car. The emergency crew at roadside looked at me, trying to reason how a human being could emerge with only a mild concussion from a pressed vehicle that appeared to have already gone through the junkyard's metal compressor. Slack-jawed and wide-eyed, they looked as if they had just seen a ghost—maybe the Holy Ghost.

So did this knucklehead (yours truly) immediately drop to his knees and thank God for saving him? "Hell no." For you Christians out there offended by my writing *hell no*, I mean it literally—hell said no.

After the accident, I remained a devoted agnostic who would rather burn in hell than sacrifice my reasoning for some make-believe God. Little did I know that God basically told hell, *You can't have him.*

Why did God save such a scoundrel? My hunch today is that He honored my sincere prayer almost two years earlier that I wanted to really know Him. Maybe, and I think probably, He honored my seeking the truth, and this was His way of preventing the devil from ensnaring me.

To further disarm my defense that all Christians are hypocrites, God placed a single Christian woman named Roxanne across from my apartment. She had never smoked, never cussed and never had sex. A teacher at a Christian school, she read her Bible daily, never lost her temper and from all accounts appeared to be the most ideal example of a believer on the face of the planet. She also never condemned people like me for their lack of faith. In fact, when she saw or heard cases of people sinning, she oftentimes became physically sick and immediately started praying for those people in love. Looking back, I could see how God was removing all my excuses.

Meanwhile, I was being groomed for an executive position with Procter & Gamble (fondly referred to as "Procter & God"). Because I attained perfect scores on the tests they issued to leadership candidates, I got placed in the headquarter city of Cincinnati after graduating from Northwestern. Yet instead of getting promoted, I got fired. In my youthful ignorance, I started several trials of one of P&G's newest breakthrough products and failed to remove the trial accounts from receiving free products. It was an honest mistake of youthful stupidity.

After a humiliating return to my parents' house, I found another job with the respected company Johnson & Johnson in the Chicago area. By then something, or someone, kept pulling at my heartstrings. Miracle of miracles, I attended a church. That may not seem commensurate with God's parting the seawater to allow Moses and the Jews to escape Egypt, but on a personal level, it most assuredly compared. This devoted agnostic was becoming soft and curious.

During a "college and career" meeting at a church, the speaker asked if anyone wished to give his or her heart to Christ. As though someone had yanked my arm, I boldly rose with my hand above my head. When I met Jesus Christ as my Lord and Savior after praying the proverbial "sinner's prayer," the skies did literally part for me to spiritually connect with Jesus. My spirit danced with joy.

Becoming born again felt like being consumed with great affection and comfort. This was my first heavenly encounter with God (my near-death experience being the second). My spiritual eyes opened to a celestial place where I could sense a grand celebration in heaven. I could sense Jesus in a spiritual reality as true as any physical reality. Mostly, I sensed an intimate connection with God. My spirit rose in communion with God.

77

Imagine yourself listening to music over the airwaves. You cannot see the musician playing from afar, yet the melody soothes your soul. You start soaking in the music. For that moment of time, you and the musician are in harmony with each other, deeply in unison. And that music stays with you as a joyful sound for the rest of your life. To me, Jesus is that musician, and His presence represents the melody that lives in my heart. I could not see Him, but I heard His music, His voice. God was no longer theoretical but alive in a real relationship.

There have been times in my life, though, when I have forgotten the melody. Pain sometimes disrupts the soothing effect of God's presence, and when it does, I turn to someone on earth who knows suffering. We can empathize with each other. We understand each other. Nothing connects like someone who understands us, warts and all.

Jesus Christ knows suffering. He endured ridicule, brutal beatings and the unfathomable torture of hanging on the cross. Suffering on this earth, a shared commonality among humans, remains central to each of our stories for a reason. None of us escapes the pangs of suffering and ultimately death. That person next to you is going through a struggle unbeknownst to you right now.

I Learned to Embrace Brokenness

I first learned to embrace brokenness as a means to drawing closer to God at a church Renee and I attended in Oakland when our children were young. The pastor's message focused on the story of Jacob in Genesis 32. Jacob feared meeting his estranged brother, Esau, who planned to meet Jacob with a hostile army of four hundred men. Jacob prayed. Then a strange man showed up and wrestled him till daybreak. At some point during this weird contest, Jacob realized that he was wrestling

God. And when God decided it was time to end the match, He dislocated Jacob's hip and demanded to be released.

In great pain, Jacob said, "I will not let you go unless you bless me" (verse 26). God pronounced this blessing on Jacob, saying: "Your name shall no longer be called Jacob ["deceiver"], but Israel ["strives with God"], for you have striven with God and with men, and have prevailed" (verse 28 ESV). Jacob then limped toward his tense reunion with Esau with a weakened body and a strengthened faith. Having wrestled with God, he knew his prayers regarding Esau would be answered.

Those who wrestle with God will end up broken to some degree. The bone may heal, but they are left with some lasting effect: at the very least, the memory of what caused the pain. The blessing arrives through an earnest encounter with God to the point of becoming raw, stripped of any pretenses, and wholly dependent on God for the answers to our fears. That is my experience.

The pastor at the Oakland church went on to say that he did not trust anyone who did not walk with a limp. I agree. Someone who can say to me, in all sincerity, "I know how hard it is," provides a breath of fresh air psychologically speaking. They get it. Friend, I get it. I know what it means when God seems nowhere to be found. I am scarred. The numerous hurts, in both my body and my relationships, produced in me a sobriety of mind. I have wrestled with God as to why certain things have happened. And it is because of those scars that I am blessed and know Jesus as my Friend and my Lord.

Perhaps because I know both pain and victory and how temporary they are, I can speak to a higher purpose through it all. As a child, I was frequently ill. As an adult, I have faced life-threatening illnesses, including cancer and serious accidents that should have killed me. Friends and family have died. I have been humiliated through job losses and lost opportunities. I am broken, and because of this brokenness, I am sensitized to the pain of others. My conversations with God are now more authentic.

Other friends have likewise suffered unthinkable trials. All of them are wonderful people with loving hearts toward God. One of them, Joe Irwin, lost both of his children—one to suicide. I could tell more stories of great suffering in the lives of people I know personally. We would need to multiply those by millions to even approximate the degree of suffering in the world. Children starve. Christians get martyred because of their faith. Diseases ravage the innocent. The list goes on.

These are the consequences of a world gone astray. Jesus forewarned us that in this world we would "have trouble." He also told us to "take heart" because He has "overcome the world" (John 16:33). Jesus was declaring that He will cover our weaknesses with His overcoming Spirit, fill us with His own victorious life and empower us to triumph over our trials with His omnipotent power.

I Learned to Love the Broken

One of our informally adopted children is Florencio, who lives in a poor community in the Philippines. He is gay. Whatever that means to you, it means little to us in comparison to our knowing this young man as a family member. Billy Graham once framed the issue when a *San Francisco Chronicle* reporter asked him, "What if you discovered your son was gay?" Dr. Graham responded, "I would love him all the more." Not so with Florencio. One member of his family spewed homophobic insults at him that were laced with profanity, exploited him as a sex worker and eventually disowned him. Even worse, he was drugged and raped by a group of men who infected him with HIV and AIDS.

It would have been simpler just to tell Florencio about the love of Christ, yet God required that we love Florencio through our actions before telling him about the love of the Father. So God gave my family and me a love for this broken man. After that, Florencio accepted Jesus Christ as his Lord and Savior because he first knew our love. Because of Florencio's brokenness, he was open to receiving the One who loves him most, Jesus the Redeemer (see Titus 2:14).

Brokenness refines us and matures us. But it takes the evidence of love from us to help heal the broken. We are the evidence of Jesus, the face of His Spirit. Had the brokenness of my daughter, Annie, not broken me, I would never have been able to love this hurting man so transparently. I am a former football player who consciously tried to avoid homosexuals as a youth to preserve my own perception of manhood. But God broke me of this insecurity.

Having gone through the trenches of suffering and seeing my loved ones suffer as well, I now have a keen discernment of what constitutes a strong believer. I can tell a mature believer from an immature believer by how the person answers the question, Why does God allow bad things to happen to good people? The immature believer struggles with the answer. The mature believer wants to help others who are suffering. Mature believers do not require an answer; they choose to *be* that answer. When first responders are called to the scene of an accident, they do not ponder why and how that travesty happened; they simply respond.

There is no Pollyannaish answer for why bad things happen. Suffering sucks. Try to reason it through—and believe me, I experienced several mind twists, seeking the answer—and you will end up with more questions. Seek after God with an earnest desire to know Him, and you will find satisfaction that all your questions have already been answered. You will have no need to understand the whys, because you are supremely loved. First John 4:18 says, "There is no fear in love. But perfect love drives out fear, because fear has to do with punishment [suffering]. The one who fears is not made perfect in love."

How did God convert a skeptical agnostic into a devotee? Because "God is love" (1 John 4:8). And I personally know Love, not the emotion but the Person. When the Person of Love indwells you, relationship with God becomes real. Jesus Christ did that for me and for you.

Finding joy is all about relationship. In fact, 75 years of scientific research confirms that relationship more than any other factor causes joy.[1] I know this because I train lots of people and have spent thousands of hours researching the topic of joy and thriving. I have written three books about the subject of thriving.

Joy is a by-product of being steeped in God's presence. Once we are saved by His grace, He commissions us to fulfill our unique purpose for His glory. That is why God placed us on this earth—not to just be joyful creatures, but to fulfill His purpose for each of us until we die.

What is *your* purpose? Discovering your purpose allows you to understand why God placed you in this world.

—4—

Finding Purpose through Pain

An oppressive rush of frigid air hit my face as I exited my car and headed to the hospital's intensive care unit. The charge nurse had called around midnight to summon me to assist with some new monitoring instruments placed at the bedside of two dying patients. The two patients lay in separate but adjoining rooms.

As I entered the first one, an eerie malaise permeated the room. It was palpable, as if death could be felt vicariously. Two people sat near the bedside, sullen, emotionless. Nothing but stark hospital accoutrements surrounded the aged catatonic man. His face, the most revealing indicator of a person's character, appeared wrinkled and entirely decrepit. Though the attached monitor told of a man on the cusp of death, the mood in that room told of a man long since dead.

After checking the monitor, I walked over to the adjoining room to find a refreshingly different story. This man also appeared comatose, and dying, but nothing else seemed similar to his neighbor. Two loved ones sat by his bedside, thanking him for the most personal acts of love. Their tears spoke of compassion that complemented the man's serene countenance. Peace. I could sense peace as plainly as the smell of flowers placed around the room—peace and, in a strange way, almost joy.

I find it amazing how we can sense our surroundings almost instantly. Perhaps a piece of music sparks some nostalgia, or a fragrance evokes emotion or we sense something entirely ethereal. Call it a sixth sense, intuition or a compilation of our experiences rolled into some type of psychological or spiritual sensor. Perhaps it is the voice of discernment expressed in the Greek word *diakrisis*, which describes being able to appraise a person or environment and to differentiate good from evil, as described in Hebrews 5:14.

The same certainty could be said of the hospital monitor's readings foretelling the two men's death. Blood pressure slowly trailing down, pulse growing weaker, blood oxygen level falling—all meant death was around the corner. When death finally arrived for them, I discovered the themes behind their disparate lives.

Because most people in that small town knew of the two gentlemen's reputations, the nurse proceeded to describe the lifestyle of the man whose death took on an oppressive visage. He caroused around town, marrying three times, and slept with countless others while living without purpose or direction. Alcohol became both his friend and confidant. Despite his success as a businessman, none could sing his praises.

Then a smile overcame the nurse's sad expression as she told me about the other man. For forty years or so, he lived with the same wife, the one by his bedside lavishing praises on him. The man lived a simple life as a father of three, manager of the local hardware store and faithful congregant of the local church. A "kind man," she said, "pretty average, but in a good way." Considering the way others described him, he had sought a purpose more enduring than himself.

The two men left this life with the vestiges of their past. Each departed following a lifetime of investments. Their earthly accomplishments faded as they passed through death's door, leaving behind not only their legacies, but the summation of their character. Even a stranger like me could readily sense these men's very different personas, and God alone knows where they went after death.

For several decades, this profound experience stuck with me as a poignant contrast of one's legacy versus one's life. And what value can or should be ascribed to one's life? That value is a measure of the extent to which a person fulfilled a noble purpose in the eyes of neighbors and of God.

Taking Stock of Your Life

Struck by my encounter with the two dying men, I began to write a mental résumé of my life. Instead of starting from the beginning, however, I worked backward from an end that had not yet been written.

My wife and I would joke about our "remember when" conversations during our youth when we spoke of our planned future as if it had already passed. "Remember when Ryan (our son) entered his manhood, and we felt so proud that there stands a godly man of strong character." We spoke these words long ago as baby Ryan lay in his crib. Since then, we have experienced the pleasure of seeing our young son grow into a person of amazing character driven by a strong Christian faith.

Sadly, the purpose God instills within our hearts and minds sometimes fades with the reality of our passing years. Growing up erases the ease of innocence and the spark of imagination until we settle for just a job or a way to "make ends meet" or end up living out someone else's purpose rather than the one God gave to each of us. Age takes away all hope of demonstrating great prowess on the athletic field. Retirement extinguishes the expectation of greater professional achievements.

At life's end, one defining question awaits: Did I live out my purpose?

By working backward from the end of our hoped-for life, we connect future desires to current circumstances. We imagine the future not based on the present but in spite of it. Try projecting your life into the future, then share what you see with a loved one. At first, the experience may seem strange, but then it will be fun. Imagining your future frees you to dream again as God beckons you to your genuine self.

Many of us dream less about achieving worldly goals and more about being the person God wants us to be. We want to live with meaning, be more loving, more Christlike, more giving, more forgiving, more joyful, more purposeful and so on. We want to honor God with the life He has given to us. And the rift between our calling and what we settle for keeps us from living a thriving life. The good news is, we can thrive today, at this very moment.

Most who find the courage to follow their calling in Christ sacrifice ambition for the purpose of serving God and others. They listen to the hearkening of their soul rather than to the sole reasoning of their mind. They place the end goal above the beginning wants. The call to Christ's truth drowns out the insecurity in their minds.

If we plan our lives from our current state or position (as most people do), we limit our plans to what appears probable based on our experiences—not on what truly is possible through Christ. In truth, we can be exceedingly truer to our soul purpose if we project our ideal forward and allow God to make our dreams a reality. Once we know God's calling upon our lives, the goal then becomes finding out how to fashion that calling, that purpose, into our reality. The journey to our purpose can begin as early as now. By taking those first steps, we begin to live out our purpose. We enter into a meaningful life inspired by the Holy Spirit.

Finding Your Soul Purpose

One of my favorite verses (and perhaps one of yours too) is Romans 8:28: "And we know that in all things God works for the good of those who love him, who have been called according to his purpose." This verse is a guarantee that whatever happens to us will ultimately turn out good. If something is not yet good, then it is not yet the end.

Many who read Romans 8:28 miss the next verse, however, which explains our calling to fulfill God's purpose: "For those God foreknew he also predestined to be conformed to the image of his Son, that he might be the firstborn among many brothers and sisters." From Romans 8:29, we know that God predestined us for the purpose of being conformed to the image of His Son, Jesus Christ.

Purposefulness defined the early Church just as it should define our lives. Keeping our relationship with God foremost in our minds and hearts translates into living intentionally with purpose. God has given you a purpose. Purpose defines your life. No one else but you can fulfill your purpose. Not fulfilling your purpose creates a vacuum in this world.

God has defined a "purposeful era" of reality wherein we focus on the question of what God has created us to do. As children of God, we thrive as God connects us to a purpose and produces good works through us. In God's purposeful era of possibilities, a bank executive becomes a corporate chaplain; an academic becomes a chef who "cooks for Christ" while sharing his faith with patrons; and an M.B.A. graduate finds his calling as a police officer who ministers to those in crisis. Such stories speak to bold soul-searchers who discount the comfortable in favor of their true destiny in Christ.

The call of truth serves as our key to open the doorway to our purpose. Christ beckons us like a beam of light through the fog of life's obstacles, opening the gateway to our truest self. When Jesus declared, "You will know the truth, and the truth will set you free" (John 8:32), He meant that truth frees us from the false perceptions that lead to just "settling" in life, allowing us to contemplate the unimaginable. You "can do all things through Christ" (Philippians 4:13 KJV).

Consider how embracing that truth could change your entire life. Whether 19 or 91 years of age, it does not matter. All of us wish for more. Whether in person or in position, we seek higher ground. And there is no better way to define our life than to make its closing chapter the beginning of a life honoring to God.

When I met Jesus, I did not hear Him tell me those words I longed for: "Well done, good and faithful servant!" (Matthew 25:21). That is because He was not yet finished with me in this world. My glimpse of heaven was just a preview. I can certainly testify to you that the comforting light of Jesus makes everything in heaven aglow with glorious colors and an abundance of life budding forth lush fields of flowers, green mountains, crystal waters and joy everlasting. Of course I wanted to stay, but Jesus made this absolutely clear to me: I could not stay in paradise without fulfilling my purpose in this world. That same edict applies to you. If your heart beats today, it is because your purpose is not yet complete. God designed specific work for you to accomplish, and only you can do it. Heaven can wait.

Our purpose was established by God as the reason for our life in this world. Not knowing our purpose can leave us joyless and hopeless. As a result, we may feel insignificant, unfocused, even worthless. Lack of purpose in this world can also, at times, make us feel as if God has abandoned us. But here is the *great* news: God has a purpose for you, "plans to prosper you and not to harm you, plans to give you hope and a future" (Jeremiah 29:11). That future is a life of good works, "for we are God's handiwork, created in Christ Jesus to do good works, which God prepared in advance for us to do" (Ephesians 2:10).

God established a purpose for each of us, which is the very reason for our life in this world. To execute a plan for each of our lives, God gives a special "voice" to each one of His children according to our makeup. Some are introverts, some are extroverts. Some are optimists, some are more evaluative. You will see life through the lens of your nature as you are "transformed by the renewing of your mind" through Christ (Romans 12:2). As a body, we exist distinct in purpose yet interdependent in fulfilling God's purpose, as Paul described in 1 Corinthians 12:12–27. Each part operates as a necessary function for the benefit of the whole body.

Some have natural talents such as craftsmanship, while others have the talent to write. Some feel a passion for camping out in the wilderness, while others thrive in the city. Some are gifted with evangelism to witness the salvation message of Christ, while others have the gift of administration or "helps." The difference between natural talents, such as artistry, and spiritual gifts, such as prophecy, is this: We are born with talents, whereas spiritual gifts are supernaturally given to believers to build up (edify) the Body of Christ and equip them for "works of service" (Ephesians 4:12).

Where our talents, passions, personality (e.g., behavioral styles) and gifts intersect is where our purpose in life lies. For example, someone who is a gifted teacher, talented communicator and an introvert might function as a writer, actor, teacher, artist or any number of positions that tap into that person's deep inner life, which lends itself toward a sincere compassion for others. Or take an extrovert who loves to help others and has the spiritual gifts of discernment and mercy. That person might serve in a counseling or leadership role for people going through mental or emotional distress. In the Church he or she may serve as a prayer intercessor. A passion for social change might drive someone to run for the local school board or enter some other form of politics.

By piecing together your natural and supernatural abilities, you find purpose in life. Your purpose may be fulfilled through a vocation, either in a secular career, in the Church, or both. A synonym for *vocation* is *calling*, which is derived from the Latin word *vocare*, meaning "to call."[1] If you are at a secular job (such as a politician), your purpose is always to shine God's light in that place so that others "may see your good deeds and glorify your Father in heaven" (Matthew 5:16). Or you might serve others in the community (e.g., by volunteering at a soup kitchen) or within the Body of Christ (e.g., by teaching Sunday school).

God's second great Commandment, "Love your neighbor as yourself" (Matthew 22:39), comes only after loving God "with all your heart and with all your soul and with all your mind" (verse 37). These constitute the two greatest Commandments Jesus gave. By studying God's Word (the Bible), by immersing ourselves in His presence (through prayer and worship), by maintaining consistent fellowship with other believers, and by obeying God, we become conformed to Christ's image. We become more Christlike.

This is how God transforms the "want to" of life (e.g., *I want to be more loving and caring*) to the "have to" of life (e.g., *I am more loving and caring—that's who I am, so it comes naturally or supernaturally to me*). Our propensity for doing good just spills out of us. When we grow in loving relationship to God, we are empowered to love other people, and this, my friends, fulfills God's *second* purpose for us: to serve others with our passions, our talents, our gifts and our personalities—and with the benefit of our experiences.

This is the all-embracing purpose for you and me—and for all believers. As we become conformed to the image of Jesus Christ, He becomes the motivation for doing good works. His Spirit transforms us from wanting to do what is good to being compelled to do good. Obedience to God implies a trust in His promises as He transforms us with His presence and His truths. God's purpose for us is Christlikeness.

What does it take to be Christlike? The essential elements are spending time with God, obeying His commands, praising and worshiping Him, and fellowshiping with other believers. Developing a relationship takes time, so we need to spend time praying and reading God's Word consistently to realize intimacy with Jesus.

In the early Church described in Acts 2:42–47, the believers devoted themselves to the apostles' teachings, fellowshiping with each other, "breaking bread" and praising God. They experienced phenomenal intimacy with God. They worshiped Him from their hearts with expressions of love, adoration, enchantment and celebration.

Defining a Purpose through a Problem

Very often our purpose is defined by a problem or crisis. In her twenties, Sheri and her toddler son, Nathan, needed a place to stay. They had nothing. "I will never forget asking my church family members if they could help," she recalls. "They offered to pray for me and offered advice, but no one actually gave me what I needed—beds and other provisions we needed to just survive." Through zealous prayer, according to Sheri's words, God began giving her visions about a safe place for women and a storehouse filled with all kinds of essentials.

Another vision, which remains clearly visible in her mind to this day, was that of a cross. God showed her "the vertical piece is the plumb line of His word—the truth. The other horizontal piece is the practical. Where needs are met." Sheri explained it from the perspective of Jesus' feeding the poor as well as teaching them. "It was the complete deal. He showed me the cross. The two intersect. They work together. When I was a single mom, the practical provisions coming to me were what I needed to feel, taste—to see the Lord is good." She chose betterment over bitterness.

At the eleventh hour, a few Christians gave Sheri what she needed. Then she used some extra cash to rent a garage and start Bridge of Hope, a ministry that provides donated clothes, furniture, cookware, food and other items to families in underprivileged areas. They served refugees from Iraq, Nepal, Vietnam, Burma, Uganda and other war-torn countries. People from all faiths and backgrounds frequented the storehouse, including Hindus, Muslims, Buddhists, Christians, local gang members, drug addicts and prostitutes—and all were welcomed enthusiastically. Word spread, and soon volunteers from all over the country contributed supplies and planned community events.

Today, Bridge of Hope operates a large warehouse within the poorest community in San Diego County, allowing them to feed thousands unable to pay for groceries. Volunteers teach English classes to foreign-speaking children and adults, music classes for those used to hearing only sirens in "the hood" and dance or art classes for those who seek to escape their desolation. The community center hosts private tutoring, after-school programs, sports camps, Alcoholics Anonymous meetings and vocational training. Families of those victimized all too often in the crime-ridden area hold funeral services there. College and university students from across the nation intern at Bridge of Hope. God used Sheri's trials as a young mother in need to turn her pain into her purpose, inspiring her to start one of the most successful charities in the world.

Followers of Christ look outside of themselves to find a problem, and the solution can define their life. They are called by a problem, and their calling forms their mission. A truly inspired physician must help the sick. A dedicated teacher must equip students with tools to succeed in life. An inspired children's caseworker must prevent abuse. Sheri Briggs started Bridge of

Hope through the hardship of homelessness, and you, too, must discover the problem you are tailored to solve.

Is there something that really bothers you—not a mere annoyance, but a grating, gnawing problem that eats away at your ability to enjoy life? Perhaps it is some terrible injustice, such as world hunger or disease or the lack of good education in high schools. As a follower of Jesus Christ, you must take action to undo what bothers you the most. The problem may be something in the neighborhood or at work that causes others to suffer or fail; or it may be a disease, shortcoming or injustice that has plagued your own life. Once you find your vocation, allow God to position you within your workstation. Make sure not to sacrifice God's commission for driving ambition. Give God permission to turn your pain into gain.

That intolerable problem will lead you to find your purpose. You need not dedicate your career toward solving that problem—you can simply do something positive by serving as a volunteer or do something else without receiving an income. However you do it, you must do it. You might try to tackle some irritating problem at work or in the neighborhood. Or you might bring food to a grieving family out of empathy from having lost a loved one. You were created to solve a problem, and your joy in life depends on your commitment to solving that problem with your talents, experiences, gifts and relationships.

Sometimes, a tragedy defines your intolerable problem. A loved one may have suffered, which compels you to help relieve others' suffering. When a problem becomes a blood-fueled living force that boils over into consistent anger or frustration, not solving it would be tantamount to being disloyal to you. If the problem of abortion gnaws at you, work at a Christ-centered crisis pregnancy center. If the problem of child abuse gnaws at your gut, become a foster parent. If God puts an invention on your heart that solves an insufferable problem, find a solution. Finding your intolerable problem and making it your life's work to solve that problem is the best way toward satisfying the purpose for which you were created.

Then confirm your purpose through others' affirmations. What do people say you are good at? Look for a common narrative or theme. Do they say you make things clear and understood? If so, you may have the gift of teaching, so teach. If they say you are great at working with your hands, then make that your hobby or vocation. If they say you inspire them with your prayers, then intercede in prayer for others. That purpose need not be a position within an organization. Being purposefully intentional means looking for opportunities to practice your purpose in the minutia of life.

When my friend went to get a haircut, the stylist shared with him that a gentleman in the chair next to him had recently lost his wife. My friend lost his wife to cancer years before, so he shared his experience and prayed with the grieving man beside him. Christians should not just hang out in life. Look for opportunities to represent the love of Jesus Christ.

Within the Body of Christ, search for ways to help your brothers and sisters. Maybe you are astute in calling attention to sin and wrong attitudes, or you can supernaturally interpret the purposes of God. If so, prophesy to others, because prophecy is a God-given gift to edify your family in Christ. If you like the outdoors, look for opportunities to work or spend more time outdoors at retreats. If your experience with something equips you with the knowledge to help others, then you must do it.

The gifts of the Spirit enable us believers to do what God has called us to do. Second Peter 1:3 says, "His divine power has given us everything we need for a godly life through our knowledge of him who called us by his own glory and goodness." The gifts of the Holy Spirit are part of that "everything we need" to fulfill His purposes for our lives. When we pursue our purpose, regardless of how large or small, God will put His super on our natural to accomplish something supernatural.

Learning about Persistence

After my daughter, Annie, was violently attacked, she, Renee, and I started a company called The Defense Shop (www .thedefenseshop.com) to supply self-defense products to people needing personal protection. At fairs, we would encounter women who had been attacked. Besides equipping these victims with products like stun guns and pepper spray to ward off potential attackers, in some cases we were able to pray with them. The more joy we gave to others, the more joy we received. The pain from Annie's attack was being turned for good.

To further our purpose, Annie, Renee and I decided to open a Defense Shop kiosk at a mall in Escondido, California. Sales were far less than we expected. This venture seemed like a loss. We questioned whether or not we had misinterpreted God's direction by pursuing this endeavor.

Then one day an inconspicuous man with crooked glasses stopped by our booth to inquire about our products. He left a business card, and we thought little of this encounter until a friend at church encouraged us to follow up with the man. We discovered this man was known as "The Entrepreneur's Best Friend." At our meeting, Renee mentioned one of her inventions, a portable pop-up pet door (www.popuppetdoor.com) that she and her sister created for our sixteen-year-old dog, Scout, so he could go outside without our needing to leave the door open. Renee created this product to solve a perplexing problem, but God used it to form a purpose far beyond a simple fix.

We formed a partnership with investors. Then we auditioned for the hit television show *Shark Tank*, and the producers selected our product to move forward. Since then, Renee has appeared on television shows and traveled around the country, promoting this multimillion-dollar product. Along the way, Renee shares her love of God by ministering to those in need.

That auspicious introduction at a little kiosk led to a supernatural success through Christ. God turned our intention into His perfection. That is the way God seems to operate. He weaves a tale of purpose through the small twists and turns of our journeys. He uses failure to help us learn, grow and connect the dots to some larger picture. We just need to take that first step and then the next and then the next one after that. And when we fall down, we need to simply get up and try again. God works in the minutia to produce the macro of our life. Our job is to follow His way and trust His providence.

The macro of my life changed dramatically six years ago when I was laid off from a medical device company, along with most of my leadership team. Now I look back on my former life and wonder why I did not lay myself off years earlier. This layoff launched my career as a full-time trainer of people. God has a way of causing major disruptions in our lives as a wake-up call to force us into heeding a higher calling. By their very definition these seminal events (getting fired, turning a certain age, the diagnosis of a serious illness, a lost relationship) influence later developments and cause us to pause, reflect and ask God, *What do You want me to do with my life now?*

After I was laid off, my search for wisdom led me to start a human development company. I now help develop people's skills and abilities while teaching leaders and believers in Jesus Christ how to thrive in life. I love it. Thanks to my passion for writing, I get to share what God is teaching me through this book and several other books, workbooks and articles.

What about you? What seminal events have helped shape your life? Any regrets? Any turning points that made things better? Perhaps God has pulled the proverbial rug out from under your feet to redirect your steps. Maybe, like me, you have discovered that someone else's rejection is God's redirection. Those seminal events force us to reconsider the path we are on, and though sometimes they are beyond our control, we should welcome them—not dread them. They make us more capable of fulfilling our dreams, aspirations and true purposes.

The key takeaway is, do not wait for that crisis to happen. Plan for it. Explore what-if scenarios to think of possibilities over probabilities. When we are confronted with any occasion to make a change via a shock or dramatic turn of events, our human tendency is to go back to what is most comfortable. And too often, the desire for the comfort of yesterday's habits tends to win out over our desire for a better future. The key to fulfilling your divinely inspired purpose is to alter your response to the seminal events that invariably happen in life. These events can turn the impossible (opportunities) into the inevitable decision points that force us to think, Why not?

Consider planning these events in advance. That is right: What would you do if you were diagnosed with a terminal illness today? What about if you were fired—then what? If you lost your closest loved one today, how would you reroute your life? What would you do in a crisis? The truth is, these events can quickly turn shoulda-couldas into reality if we do not simply look for another replacement that is much the same (i.e., *if I lost my job, I would get another job in the same field*). Discover what you would do after a seminal event (or crisis) and flip that scenario into a potential plan for releasing the dream that God once placed in your heart.

Instead of trying to return to the past, accept the fact that sameness is never really the same. We can never fully go back. The truth is, that job you were laid off from was not really that great anyway, so consider avoiding taking another similar position. Maybe God wants to use you to make a bigger impact. Awaken yourself to a new perceptual reality of what you can do through Christ if the foundation beneath you suddenly evaporated.

These seminal events are finite—do not waste them. They present the pivotal points God uses to redirect our lives. Seminal shocks, seemingly daunting adventures, changes, risks and stretch goals (goals that make you stretch beyond your current goals) are all challenges. There is a direct relationship between challenges and growth: more challenge, more growth. One cannot happen without the other, just as we cannot strengthen our muscles without bodily resistance.

If we learn from these lessons and apply our newfound understanding or perspective, we can create a more meaningful plan for anything we do. As challenges happen, we can seek God's wisdom to grow. We can strengthen our ability to plan more effectively with purpose. Likewise, being purposeful allows us to plan more intentionally and prevents us from simply surviving such that life is not something that just happens to us.

I pray that you will intentionally plan for God's redirections in your life. Ask yourself:

- How might God use me in a greater way?
- How might planning for seminal moments open possibilities for God to fulfill my dreams?
- How might God's redirection through a planned seminal moment bring me closer to Him and to my ultimate purpose in this life?
- How might I live more intentionally by looking for opportunities to help others?

Whatever you do in this life, "do it all for the glory of God" (1 Corinthians 10:31), working at it "with all of your heart" as though you were working for God and not just for your boss or anyone else (Colossians 3:23), for this is the will of God for your life.

When God causes seminal events in our lives, He is bringing us to our next phase in life. That next phase will sometimes involve following a bigger purpose than we have allowed ourselves to envision. As I have adapted to my seminal events, I have learned that God wants more of me, which is why He redirected me to a vocational shift: (1) so I could serve out my purpose more fully, perhaps even more intentionally than ever before, and (2) so I would grow closer to being who God wants me to be.

Your dreams need not include some grandiose plan to become noteworthy. Rather, they evoke passion within us as we imagine them. The desire to realize the dream may even draw you to tears. So rekindle your dreams. Your ability to thrive in life requires it.

Living Your Purpose Day by Day

My good friend Wayne Miller suffered from an excruciatingly painful type of bone cancer that caused him to lose six inches in height. Wayne promised me when I was a young single man that if I ever got married, he would attend my wedding. He made that promise just after receiving the prognosis from doctors that he would live no longer than three months.

Three years later, Wayne showed up with his tracheostoma (a hole or stoma in his trachea) and back brace to stand up for my wedding against the backdrop of waterfalls pounding the mountain cliffside arching above Yosemite Valley. Two weeks later, Wayne died. His wife, Libby, informed me that Wayne had literally got up off his deathbed and checked out of the hospital in Seattle so he could travel almost two thousand miles to fulfill his promise to attend my wedding.

God gave Wayne the strength and the time to bless my marriage at the end of his life, and his example of fortitude has helped me to endure my own trials. While I spoke at Wayne's "home-going," the Holy Spirit gave me a radiant vision of Wayne running along the mountain trails—six inches taller than before. God heals His children—always. And tucked inside our pain and suffering is a purpose that allows us to encourage others and "comfort those in any trouble with the comfort we ourselves receive from God" (2 Corinthians 1:4).

I often think back on Wayne's perseverance as a model for my own life. In fact, he helped inspire me on a mission to develop the skills anyone can apply toward realizing an abundant life. My thirty-year research project about the thriving mindset uncovered the four foundations for a thriving life:

- Purpose
- Attitude
- Connection
- Energy

Undergirding all these foundations is a strong relationship with Jesus Christ and other loved ones. Based on a study of over fourteen thousand people, the absolute requirement for thriving in life is intimacy with Christ. Our worst situations typically happen when someone or something distances us from our relationship with Jesus, such as people or calamities that pull our attention away from God.[2]

If you asked me to identify the worst situation I experienced, the one that most challenged my thriving life, this would be my answer: the one I found myself in during the moment it occurred. The rest of them I got through.

I survived death. I survived the deaths of loved ones. I survived seeing my children and loved ones suffering when I could do nothing but pray. I survived having no money and nowhere to find it. I have been hired, fired, promoted, demoted, upsized, downsized, greedy, needy, the top dog and the bottom dog. I survived heart failure, excruciating pain from surgeries, and life-threatening cancer.

When my doctor called me on a Friday night and informed me that radiology tests had discovered a growth on my lung,

I clicked off the cell phone and sat in my car, staring at the dashboard with my heart racing. This was nine years after I experienced my NDE. I have faced cancer threats three times. Surgery removed spots for two of them.

I understand the trepidation that arises moments before the doctor enters the room to reveal the lab results, telling of health or disease. I know the inevitable anguish therein. We imagine the worst and pray for the best. The news, either positive or negative, seems almost anticlimactic compared to the panic swirling in the mind.

In the case of the spot on my lung, I went to the doctor after my third radiogram. My pulmonologist walked into the room, turned the computer screen to show me the image and pointed to where the spot had been located. It was gone. We could determine no other reason for its disappearance than that it was not yet my time. My purpose had yet to be fulfilled. Today I am cancer-free. Tomorrow—only God knows. There is no promise of tomorrow (see James 4:13–14).

Should I have been immunized to suffering and death? No.

Did God delight in my suffering? No way. Heredity or some other factor in this disease-laden world caused it.

But I was caught in a frightening moment, thinking I might die slowly from cancer. What happened subsequently is that God used this trial to bring me closer to Him, and I learned the power of fervent prayer. Everything I have been through has led to my ultimate purpose of helping others find purpose and thrive regardless of their stage in life.

For me, the essential question is, What will I do today?

Friends, today each one of us is living his or her purpose. We are alive on this earth for a reason—to serve God while being conformed to Christ's image. What an amazing calling we have in Christ. That makes for a thriving and purposeful life, one moment and one person at a time.

—5—

Knowing God As a Friend

Knowing God is more about relationship than it is about faith. Faith allows us to believe in the unseen, serving as a bridge through which we receive Jesus Christ as our Lord and Savior (see Ephesians 2:8–9). Intimate relationship with God, however, requires much more. Our goal should be to reach *koinonia*, deep fellowship, with God—much more than the warm fuzzy feeling we gain from being with someone. The Greek word *koinonia* occurs seventeen times in the New Testament. For instance, Paul encourages us to have "the fellowship of the Holy Spirit" (2 Corinthians 13:14) and "common sharing in the Spirit" (Philippians 2:1). Koinonia means a deep empathy with Christ's sufferings (see Philippians 3:10).

When we achieve a koinonia relationship with God, we feel as Jesus feels. We know each other profoundly. Faith is "confidence in what we hope for and assurance about what we do not see" (Hebrews 11:1). Koinonia is a deep connection with God. The closer we get to God, the more joy we experience in His presence (see Psalm 21:6), irrespective of our circumstances.

Believing in God establishes trust; koinonia with God results in transformation. Just as closeness with other people makes us more like them, so getting close to Jesus Christ makes us more like Him. It also draws us to a deeper knowledge of how intensely God loves us.

God loves you more than you can possibly comprehend. Love is the basis of all close bonds. Of the three lasting essentials Paul lists in 1 Corinthians 13:13—faith, hope and love—the greatest is love. The other two, faith and hope, cannot be realized without a loving relationship with God. Love is the essence of God, and our born-anew spirit was brought to life through the love Christ imparted to us (see 1 Corinthians 15:22).

In heaven, I experienced koinonia with Jesus, in that He and I were of one heart. To say it was amazing would be a gross understatement. I knew then, as I know now, that God desires a level of intimacy with us that centers us with each other in absolute kinship. When we are intimate with Jesus, nothing else matters. I tear up even thinking about it.

I also know that God does not want us to wait until heaven for that sense of koinonia. He wants us to be ever-present with Him. Perhaps that is what impressed me most about my heavenly experience with Jesus. God wants to "hang out" with you. If you want a profound encounter with God, you need to spend consistent time with Him as Paul described in 1 Thessalonians 5:16–18: "Rejoice always, pray continually, give thanks in all circumstances; for this is God's will for you in Christ Jesus." This translates into communicating with the Spirit of God when you are shopping, working, driving, watching television—anywhere you live and breathe.

Ask God for direction, wisdom or anything you need to live according to your God-ordained purpose, and He will give it to you (see Matthew 7:7). You can talk with God about little stuff as well as about the big stuff. Most of all, ask God to draw you closer to Him and then expect Him to do it, because the evidence of faith is not hope but expectancy. Expect God to deliver on His promises, then look for His delivery in unexpected places. Expectancy happens in anticipation of God's faithfulness through an earnest desire to know Him.

Drawing close to God requires *total* immersion in His presence. David's pursuit of God was tireless. Even when being pursued by His enemies, David did not seek victory; He sought God with *all* his heart. He wrote in Psalm 63:1: "You, God, are my God, earnestly I seek you; I thirst for you, my whole being longs for you, in a dry and parched land where there is no water."

The apostle Paul considered "everything a loss because of the surpassing worth of knowing Christ Jesus my Lord, for whose sake I have lost all things. I consider them garbage, that I may gain Christ" (Philippians 3:8). To Paul the foremost relationship was intimacy with his Lord. God consumed Paul's focus and desires. Becoming a friend with God entails a consuming desire for intimacy. The more we know God, the more we want to know Him. Paul continued, "I want to know Christ—yes, to know the power of his resurrection and participation in his sufferings, becoming like him in his death" (verse 10).

My most intimate times with God have been when I got still with God (see Psalm 46:10) by slowing the busyness of life. When that happens, God invites me into His presence, and my spirit says, *Yes!* There are several verses about spending time with God. These are three of my favorites:

[God says,] "Call to me and I will answer you and tell you great and unsearchable things you do not know."

Jeremiah 33:3

[David says,] "How lovely is your dwelling place, LORD Almighty! My soul yearns, even faints, for the courts of the LORD."

Psalm 84:1–2

Jesus says, "I am the vine; you are the branches. If you remain in me and I in you, you will bear much fruit; apart from me you can do nothing."

John 15:5

Psalm 22:3 says that the King of kings is "enthroned on" our praises (NLT). Wherever we worship God with our praises, we become a habitation for His presence. God comes to dwell with us, and when that happens, He brings His presence. The word *presence* is almost always translated from the Hebrew *paneh* or *paniym*, meaning "face."[1] Jesus literally faces us with His person, His power and His love. And where the Spirit of God is present with us, the borders of hell's domain are shoved away from us to give room to the joy, peace and hope Paul referred to in Romans 15:13 describing the power of the Holy Spirit.

Jesus gave us the Lord's Prayer to illustrate how we can be captivated by God's Spirit (see Matthew 6:9–13). The prayer begins with worshiping God: "Our Father in heaven, hallowed be your name" (verse 9). Then verse 10 extends an invitation for His Kingdom to come and His will to "be done on earth as it is in heaven." When we glorify God, we are reaching into the invisible realm to welcome the entry of His divine authority so we can meet face-to-face in the hallowed space of communion with God. Through prayer, we are inviting God's established will to be manifested in our life on earth. He takes control.

The Wonder of Koinonia

After much earnest prayer, my third profound encounter with Jesus Christ occurred during a men's retreat in Lake Tahoe following some worship, teaching, prayer and a rich night of camaraderie. The winter air outside was crisp and the ground fluffy white with snow. Inside the large living room where we had gathered, the fireplace crackled, and the thinly carpeted floor invited us to bend our knees in prayer. Reverent silence filled the room.

There, my intimacy with Christ rivaled my time with Him in heaven, minus the distinct senses of touch, sight and hearing I experienced during my NDE. This time my spirit communed with God through the senses of assurance, ethereality and knowing—as impressions, rather than the vision I experienced in heaven with Jesus. It began as we spent quiet time just dwelling with our Lord. In complete stillness, while silently praising my Father for all of His blessings, I became overwhelmed with God's love.

The generosity of His mercy and grace brought me to tears and magnified my praises to God. I asked my Lord to increase the depth and breadth of my thanksgiving to Him such that my praises would echo through heaven unto His throne. The Lord then opened my spiritual ears to hear those praises enjoined by angels, and the sound swelled my soul to overflowing. I was immersed in God the Father's presence. I was struck with wonder, and my muscles tensed as I felt utterly safe and protected.

A note will help explain what I experienced. There is a difference between the familiar, brotherly relationship believers know with Jesus (see Hebrews 2:11; Romans 8:29; Mark 3:34) and what I experienced near death during my time with Jesus and the mighty awe, respect and submission evoked in relationship to the glory of Father God (see Psalm 103:13; Deuteronomy 6:24; Proverbs 19:23; Revelation 11:18). The Godhead is comprised of God the Father, Jesus the Son and the Holy Spirit, all of whom are referred to as God (see Titus 2:13; Acts 5:3–4). These three Persons of God are perfectly united in their goal of saving and sustaining us (see 1 John 5:7; Hebrews 9:14), and each maintains a distinct role in the Godhead (see 2 Corinthians 13:14). Jesus is called "God" (*theos*) several times in the New Testament (John 1:1; 20:28; Titus 2:13; Hebrews 1:8; 2 Peter 1:1; Isaiah 9:6). So while there is no difference in authority among the three members of the Godhead, there *is* a difference in their characteristics.

In that room with those other men, I felt the almightiness of the Father described in Psalm 24:8 as the "King of glory . . . strong and mighty" and the reverence inspired by Isaiah's proclamation that "Yahweh is the everlasting God, the Creator of the whole earth. He never grows faint or weary" (Isaiah 40:28 HCSB). My sense of the Father was reflected in the New Testament reference to Him as the *pantokrator*, the all-powerful One (see 2 Corinthians 6:18; Revelation 1:8; 4:8; 11:17; 15:3; 16:7, 14; 19:6, 15; 21:22).[2] The Father literally holds everything, whereas the Son was "appointed heir of all things" (Hebrews 1:2). They are equal in their divine attributes, but in that place, I sensed the glory of the Father. There was a distinct difference between my encounter with Jesus as my body neared death at the hospital three years earlier and my encounter with Him at the men's retreat in Lake Tahoe. Jesus spoke to me with an assuring whisper, God the Father spoke with a declarative roar, and the Holy Spirit continually spoke with me as an enlightened "Comforter" (John 14:26 KJV).

It is important to understand these differences as I describe what followed in that room. The weight of the Father's love pressed me to the ground in holy adoration. My body fell to the floor, where I lay prostrate and paralyzed. I felt no fear, but I did feel God's power and love. While I was in awe of the Father, the Holy Spirit began to impart a warmth throughout my body. I had no sense of time, but my brothers in Christ later said that I had been lying on the floor for about forty minutes. During that time, my spirit worshiped the Father, praising Him from the depth of my soul. I knew that I was on hallowed ground and dared not move. The immense gravity of being in the Father's presence commanded every heavenly being to focus solely on the magnificence of the Father.

When I awoke, the Spirit of God almighty possessed me with absolute conviction and power. I began prophesying to some of the men in the room, and one young man dropped to his knees in tears as I declared God's freedom over him (I later discovered that he had been mentally and sexually abused for most of his childhood). It literally felt as though I could draw the fire out of the fireplace without burning anyone, such that the immersive fire of the Father would engulf everyone with God's holiness. I began declaring God's authority over all kinds of powers and principalities in the name of Jesus Christ according to Matthew 18:18. The men in the room froze, as this once reserved and conservative man (me) spoke like a wild person. I was completely unlike myself. That is the power of our Father.

When I finished speaking the Father's authority over the men, my body went limp and I felt drunk. My speech was slurred. I wobbled around the room, giggling like a five-year-old while placing my hand on men's shoulders and saying, "Bless you," "God loves you so much," and so forth. By then, the authoritative voice of Father God in freeing others had been replaced with the soothing voice of the Holy Spirit to pronounce comfort and love to all. Keep in mind that this behavior was completely out of character for me, a reserved introvert.

The same thing happened to the believers in the early Church when the Holy Spirit fell on them. The apostle Peter assured the crowd that the disciples were drunk with the Spirit and not alcohol: "These people are not drunk, as you suppose. It's only nine in the morning!" (Acts 2:15).

After the group adjourned, it took three men to carry me to my SUV. Of course, I could not drive—I was drunk in the Spirit. So one of my brothers drove me to our family's cabin in Lake Tahoe. "Big Dan," as we called him, placed me on my bed and asked me if I would be okay.

"Of course, my gracious brother," I replied. "God loves *you* and so do I!" I chuckled with a joyful abandonment.

Left alone in that room, I began to praise God. I was back with Jesus, the same familiar person I met in heaven. I could sense Him in my spirit as plainly as I could see Him after losing consciousness in the hospital years before. I could see both my physical surroundings and a faint visage of Jesus in the bedroom. I could also faintly see two towering angelic figures on either side of my bed. My spiritual eyes had been opened just as God opened the eyes of a young man as described in 2 Kings 6:17, allowing me to see into the spiritual realm. I asked the angels a question, but one of the angels replied: *Do not speak to us; speak only to your Lord.* By the way, these angels were freakishly big.

I continued having a conversation with Jesus as though we were two friends making small talk. I felt no need to ask any profound questions such as, Why do You allow suffering? Instead, I said things such as, "Jesus, I just love You so much!" And He would respond with something like, *And My love for you is beyond anything you could ever imagine.*

I zigzagged over to the bathroom sink to brush my teeth while continuing our familiar conversation. "Lord, why do You show up to me like this?" I asked.

Because I love you, He answered. *Trust me always.* His responses were as simple as that. He gave no scholarly answers. Jesus simply wanted to be with me and I with Him. We were being chums with each other, kicking back like two close friends.

There was one message of grand importance that I knew I must share with others, and it is this:

When My children hear My voice, they often deny it for lack of understanding. They reason with their minds what cannot be reasoned, for no one can understand the fullness of My love or My way, though they know Me because I am. I require obedience and trust, not understanding. My word speaks truth, and those who obey My truth will know Me.

I stayed up until about four in the morning, just talking with Jesus. Now, I know that some may want to hear every word spoken, but if I were to share what remains special to me, you would probably be disappointed with how mundane it might seem. And that is because being in koinonia with the Spirit of Jesus Christ is like being with someone "who sticks closer than a brother" (Proverbs 18:24). Spending time with Him is both familiar and profound at the same time—and it is unique to you and me. He speaks to you in ways that are specially tailored to you just as He spoke with me in ways specific to what I needed to hear. That is how God works. He speaks to the needs of each of His children in a voice singular to them.

The following day, I was not tired from lack of sleep, but I did experience a hangover without the headache or any other negative effect. It was a pleasant buzz. I called my wife to share the experience, and she was amazed at how excited and relaxed I seemed over the phone. "I can't wait to hear all about it when you get back," she said. The truth is, I could not possibly share everything that happened with Jesus in that space between heaven and earth. The men at the retreat wanted to hear what it was like to be slain in the Spirit and made drunk in His presence, but at that time I could not possibly put into words the magnitude of what happened.

Lessons from My Time with Jesus

During my time with Jesus, I learned something about my purpose: to bring hope to the hopeless so that each of us can live life to the fullest in intimacy with God. That is why I wrote this book and why I have written three other books about thriving in life. I also learned this profound insight: The Father's presence is mighty (awesome), Jesus Christ's presence is familiar, and the Holy Spirit's presence is entirely comforting. And each part comprises the whole of God.

Most of the time when we are communicating with God, it is through the Holy Spirit, who

- speaks (see Acts 8:29; 2 Peter 1:21)
- witnesses (see Hebrews 10:15)
- helps (John 14:16)
- teaches (see John 14:26)
- advocates (see John 14:16–17; 15:26–27; 16:7)
- guides (see John 16:13)

The three persons of God speak with one voice according to their Kingdom function. God the Father is preeminently the Creator, Jesus is the Redeemer, and the Holy Spirit is the Sanctifier ("blesser"). Even though all three operate together in all ways as one Body of God, they remain distinct.

The conundrum in understanding the nature of God results in our trying to fit God into our perception of reality. We try to reason with God, and yet no one knows the mind of the Lord (see Romans 11:34). Suffice it to say, "In the beginning was the Word, and the Word was with God, and the Word was God" (John 1:1). There are three important things in this passage about Jesus and the Father:

1. Jesus was "in the beginning"—He was present at Creation. Jesus has existed forever with God.
2. Jesus is distinct from the Father—He was "with" God.
3. Jesus is the same as God in nature—He "was God."

Beyond that, there is no need to further reason with God. What is important is that we know Him as a friend. God created you in His image so that He could have a personal relationship with you. God desires a heart-to-heart (koinonia) relationship with you that is familiar, not distant. God is your Father, but He also desires friendship with you. The Bible commonly refers to Abraham as the patriarch of the Jewish people, and he was called "God's friend" (James 2:23).

God is like any loving parent, although infinitely more so. You can trust Him as your friend and someone you can approach with any problem or struggle or failure, and He will give you protection and a safe place in which to rest (see Psalm 91:1–2). God wants to be that kind of friend to you. Jesus calls us His friends in John 15:12–17:

> "My command is this: Love each other as I have loved you. Greater love has no one than this: to lay down one's life for one's friends. You are my friends if you do what I command. I no longer call you servants, because a servant does not know his master's business. Instead, I have called you friends, for everything that I learned from my Father I have made known to you. You did not choose me, but I chose you and appointed you so that you might go and bear fruit—fruit that will last—and so that whatever you ask in my name the Father will give you. This is my command: Love each other."

When we have a conversation with God, both parties talk and listen. Because God is God, He is not confined to one way of talking to you. In the Bible, He communicated through a "whirlwind" (Job 38:1 NLT), an earthquake (see Exodus 19:18), and a voice like thunder (see 1 Samuel 2:10; Job 37:2; Psalm 104:7; John 12:29). But in this age of grace, God speaks more softly. His voice may sound like spontaneous words that seem right with your heart.

I have often been awoken in the middle of the night thinking about someone, and God has taught me that He places someone or something on my mind so I can pray for that person or thing. This voice could be in the form of an impression, as when your conscience is troubled or at peace. The voice of God speaks with peace and assurance. His messages are pure, gentle, reasonable, merciful and beneficial (see James 3:17). By contrast, "bitter envy and selfish ambition" do not come down from God;

they are "earthly, unspiritual, demonic" (verses 14–15). The voices of demons speak with confusion, lust, anxiety, jealousy, doubt and fear.

God speaks to us in the stillness of our souls as we remain silent before Him. In Psalm 62:5 David wrote, "Yes, my soul, find rest in God; my hope comes from him." Trying to listen to God when we are frantic or consumed with busyness only clouds His words with our thoughts. Koinonia usually happens for me after I have praised and worshiped the Lord either by myself or with others.

Ways to Hear God's Voice

An undistracted focus on God opens the "spiritual airwaves" for God to flow His words into our spirits. My wife and I have amazing times with the Holy Spirit. He oftentimes will speak to us with either a knowing or with an interpretation after one of us speaks in a prayer language, commonly referred to as tongues (see 1 Corinthians 14:27).

At times, I just cannot find the words to express what I wish to say with my Lord. During those times, I will speak privately in a foreign tongue that even I do not understand, trusting that God understands the expression of my spirit to Him. I do not understand the words, but I do sense the sentiment of those words as relief, comfort, peace and confidence.

As evidence that speaking in tongues exists today, Jesus told His disciples, "They will speak with new tongues" (Mark 16:17). No matter how someone explains Jesus' words theologically, His statement is an affirmation of speaking in tongues. I will leave it to those much smarter than I am to determine exactly what Jesus meant by this statement. I simply take His statement at face value. Jesus never said that these "new tongues" would be limited to public forums—to the exclusion of private worship and devotion.

Paul affirmed speaking in tongues as an act of private prayer when he encouraged the believers at Corinth to "pursue love, and desire spiritual gifts, but especially that you may prophesy" (1 Corinthians 14:1 NKJV). In verse 2, he provides guidelines for its use in public worship: "For he who speaks in a tongue does not speak to men but to God, for no one understands him; however, in the spirit he speaks mysteries" (NKJV). Paul spent the remainder of the chapter contrasting the gift of prophecy with the gift of tongues, then instructed them, "Do not forbid speaking in tongues" (verse 39)—publicly or privately.

Speaking to God is the most fundamental definition of prayer. Indeed, speaking in tongues as practiced among believers at Corinth included a different language—speaking to God, not people (see verse 2). Paul further explained in verse 2 that while believers pray (that is, speaking to God, not to any other person), no one understands them, because they speak mysteries in the spirit. This type of prayer must be done privately, Paul taught, and he forbids this type of prayer without interpretation in a public assembly in verses 27–28. Assuredly, there was a place for using tongues in the public setting and then again in the private setting in prayer.

My reason for spending time on this subject is only so that you can use the full measure of God's gifts to communicate with Him the deeper things of your spirit when words alone may not be adequate. I have personally found my prayer language (in tongues) to be very special.

Wherever and however I pray, I always ask God to possess me with His Holy Spirit, including my ears, tongue and thoughts, then I trust that what I hear or speak is genuinely inspired. All the while I check what I have heard against Scripture to make sure I am not misinterpreting what God is saying. At the same time, I continually trust in God to check my thoughts and interpretations when I ask Him to do so.

King David listened to God this way. Acts 2:25 records David as saying: "I saw the Lord always in my presence; for He is at my right hand, so that I will not be shaken" (NASB). Each of us, like David, can hear God's voice through the portals of our hearts.

Sometimes we discount God's voice as only imagination. Paul encouraged the Ephesians by praying "that the eyes of your heart may be enlightened in order that you may know the hope to which he has called you, the riches of his glorious inheritance in his holy people" (Ephesians 1:18). That God-inspired vision that seems like imagination may in fact be the childlike faith Jesus referenced when He said, "The Kingdom of God belongs to those who are like these children" (Luke 18:16 NLT). Perhaps that is why children, far more than adults, are prone to speaking of Jesus and angels in familiar terms.

As children both my son and daughter used to tell me that they saw Jesus and angels as though these visions were an everyday occurrence. Throughout the Bible God gave dreams and visions, and He said that in the last days He would pour out His Spirit and we would "dream dreams" and "see visions" (Acts 2:17). So why should we question our godly inspiration?

It is also very important for our growth and maturity that we receive some form of regular counseling and accountability through church and small groups and with Christian mentors. The Bible says that in the mouth of two or three witnesses, every fact is to be established (see 2 Corinthians 13:1). Also, with many advisors you will succeed in your walk with Christ (see Proverbs 15:22). Make sure you complement the time you spend with God with time spent with His children in fellowship and counsel.

Finally, and critically important, God's voice can be heard through the Bible, and knowing the Word of God builds faith (see Romans 10:17). When we know Scripture by heart, we can hear His voice in our heart of hearts. Knowing the Bible establishes a verifiable confidence that what we hear in our spirits is indeed the truth. We are commanded to meditate on Scripture "day and night" (Joshua 1:8).

As we read certain verses, they will resonate in our hearts as a direct message from God. Routine scriptural meditation is commanded by God and is vital to living a mature Christian life. A daily discipline of reading the Bible should be as routine as eating breakfast, lunch or dinner; and now that we have apps to keep God's Word top of mind, there is no excuse for not opening God's "love letters" to His children.

Knowing how to hear the voice of God and then spending time talking with Him and listening to His voice will enrich your life like nothing else. God wants to spend time with you. He does not want a superficial relationship with you. He wants koinonia with you.

One of my favorite unbiblical quotes comes from J. M. Barrie, the author of the children's story *Peter Pan*. He wrote: "The moment you doubt whether you can fly, you cease forever to be able to do it."[3] Start believing you can "fly," as in hearing God's voice within your heart, so you can soar in His Spirit and feel the joy of the Lord in your heart.

—6—

The Power

My intimacy with God has taught me a very important lesson: We need God's power to thrive in this frequently challenging life. Without God's power, our life yields to the draining pressures of a flawed and demanding world. Through Jesus, He released that power to overcome the powers of darkness in this world.

In His first public ministry appearance, after His forty-day fast and victory over Satan's temptations in the desert, Jesus said,

> "The Spirit of the Lord is on me, because he has anointed me to proclaim good news to the poor. He has sent me to proclaim freedom for the prisoners and recovery of sight for the blind, to set the oppressed free, to proclaim the year of the Lord's favor."
>
> Luke 4:18–19

Jesus was referencing the destruction of Satan's works, chief among them being Satan's use of his messengers—unclean spirits or demons—to oppress, harass and destroy human beings.

Twice Jesus spoke of the power God would send us in the form of the Holy Spirit. The first time, before the cross, He said to His disciples: "I am going to send you what my Father has promised [i.e., the Holy Spirit]; but stay in the city until you are clothed with *power* from on high" (Luke 24:49, emphasis added). Then, after His resurrection, Jesus told them, "You will receive power when the Holy Spirit comes on you" (Acts 1:8), which eventually happened on the Day of Pentecost. Both times, Jesus was referencing a special power essential for witnessing Christ to people and for empowering believers to fulfill their purpose.

When the Holy Spirit fills you with power, a conviction of purpose enables you to change lives and to fight the dark forces of this world. The Holy Spirit speaks to us and equips us to fulfill God's purpose through us despite the obstacles in our midst. The Holy Spirit also conforms us to the image of Christ and gives us the power to thrive and to enact our singular purpose in this life, free of the oppression influenced by invisible forces.

Jesus knew that He would no longer be walking alongside His followers once He ascended to His rightful place in heaven (see John 16:7). He also knew that God the Father is the supreme ruler who nevertheless shares in the divinity with Jesus and the Holy Spirit (see Matthew 28:18–19). Our relationship with Father God is mediated through Jesus Christ (see 1 Timothy 2:5). God the Father and God the Son are one (see John 14:8–11), but our constant fellowship with God is through the Holy Spirit, who indwells and empowers us. We are "temples of the Holy Spirit" (1 Corinthians 6:19), who abides in us as a constant companion.

Our power to thrive in this life comes from the Holy Spirit, who teaches us (see John 14:26; Luke 12:12; 1 John 2:27), speaks to us (see John 8:26), and brings us peace (see John 14:27). When I pray, I speak in the name of Jesus Christ, who said that He has given us "the keys of the kingdom of heaven" (Matthew 16:19), and I thank my Father God for loving me as His child.

I pray to one God. Then I pray asking my Lord Jesus Christ to possess me with His Spirit. It matters not the order or even the mention of each member of the Godhead. What matters is the sincerity of prayer.

In the hospital, as my breathing began to cease at the cusp of death, I can tell you that I did not have the peace of mind to say anything other than "God help me!" Instinctively I just pleaded with God to stop the suffering. My prayers spoke from the rawness of my condition. After God answered my prayer in the most profound way possible, I understood that God appreciates unvarnished prayers. There are no facades in heaven—everyone and everything is genuine.

Now I know that God manifests Himself most boldly through our cries. There is power in being real.

God Healed Our Son

Asking God to possess us with His Spirit and then trusting Him by taking hold of our Kingdom authority is the means through which the Holy Spirit releases His power through us, creating peace and sometimes causing miracles. My first miraculous experience of calling upon that power to "move mountains" happened when my son, Ryan, was in his mother's womb.

We were alarmed that our baby rolled within Renee's tummy but did not kick like a normal baby. Renee and I went in for an ultrasound at 23 weeks, expecting to hear the joyful sounds of our baby's beating heart. The ultrasound technician moved her probe in several directions. We could see our son's beating heart and rejoiced at its sound. Then a grimace crossed the technician's face.

"What's wrong?" I asked.

The technician said nothing but instead picked up a phone and cupped her hands over the speaker end while whispering something into it. Within minutes, our obstetrician (OB) entered the room. The technician turned the monitor so we could not see it. Then the OB took the probe and began rubbing it across Renee's abdomen. The technician and the OB stared at each other. Renee looked at me, her eyes tight.

The OB looked at Renee, then me, and said, "I want to show you something." He turned the screen back where we could see it. "Here's the spine." He moved his finger down the tiny rows of vertebrae. "And right here," he said, "there is a cleft or opening." What I saw was a black spot. My first thought was it had to be an equipment or user error, but then the doctor told us, "The lab test was positive for a high level of fetoprotein. It appears your baby has spina bifida."

Renee and I fixed our eyes on each other, then on the OB. "Are you sure?" she asked.

"Yes," the doctor replied. "Let's check in a few days, but in the meantime, I think you should prepare yourself."

On our way home, neither of us spoke a word. My thoughts were consumed with the possibility of lifelong care for a disabled child. At home, we reviewed the recorded ultrasound and looked at the spinal gap over and over—at least I watched it. Renee stayed silent for the most part.

That Friday afternoon we sat on the sofa next to each other and prayed. We continued praying all weekend. We sent requests to our brothers and sisters in Christ, asking them to pray with us. Then we called the *700 Club* prayer line, and a prayer warrior interceded on our behalf.

"You will not steal this child, Satan!" she declared. "You will let go of this child, and you will not rob this couple of their joy or their child's joy!" If ever we needed someone to intercede with fire on our behalf, it was that night. God divinely appointed the right intercessor at the exact time we called the *700 Club* prayer line.

As the hours passed, our prayers intensified. We confronted the demonic forces trying to steal our joy, saying, "In the name of Jesus, you must release your grip on our son and family right now! Now, God, we release Your healing touch upon our child!"

I want to emphasize that for much of the time, we prayed with righteous anger, binding the powers and principalities that were trying to rob us of our son's life and purpose. We declared Christ's authority in stopping them from carrying out their dastardly deeds. Our anger was directed entirely at the fallen angels (demons) and principalities of this world that caused this travesty. We literally prayed all day and night throughout the weekend without any fatigue.

That Sunday night, we went to a Mario Murillo healing and worship service at a church, and as the worship team began to sing and praise God, Renee felt our baby kick within her midriff for the first time. Later that night, a peace and confidence spread within our souls. A quietness replaced our angst. God controlled a space where powers and principalities once reigned. Somehow, we knew that His will had been done on earth as in heaven (see Matthew 6:10).

The following week we went back to the hospital for a follow-up ultrasound. The OB took in a deep breath before applying gel to the probe and placing it on Renee's abdomen. He looked at Renee and me with a stern expression. He continued to move the probe all around and back and forth. His entire face opened—wide eyes, gaping mouth and taut skin.

Renee and I turned to each other, bracing for the news.

The OB stopped to look up. "His spine is perfect."

As those words began to soak in, we asked, "You mean there's no spinal deformity?"

"That's correct," he replied.

Our son, Ryan, had been supernaturally healed. His healing was later documented in a book with copies of the before-and-after ultrasounds as proof, along with the physician's testimony. The only plausible explanation was that God had reached His holy hand within Renee's womb and filled the void within Ryan's spine. Today Ryan is a strapping athlete, strong and able-bodied—a living testimony of God's power and authority.

More Miracles Followed

As news spread of Ryan's healing, people asked me to pray for them. Sometimes they walked away healed; other times they did not. In particular, I remember the case of Kyle, a five-year-old boy suffering from late-stage cancer, who was bedridden and given only weeks to live. In the car, before visiting Kyle, Renee and I prayed fervently, asking God to cleanse us from all unrighteousness and to possess us with His Holy Spirit. When our confidence reached the point where we believed the Holy Spirit had indeed taken possession of us, we walked toward the hospital.

When Renee and I entered Kyle's hospital room, we witnessed his deep-set eyes, his skin wrapped around his bones with no visible fat or muscle between them. The Lord told me to ask Kyle if he wanted to meet Jesus. He said yes in a weak but confident tone.

I led Kyle in prayer as he asked Jesus Christ to take control of his life. I looked at this small emaciated boy who by now was too weak to walk, knowing that he lay within the loving embrace of Jesus. His bones protruded through his flesh, blue veins crisscrossing his bald head, and yet he smiled like any other boy.

About a week later, Renee called me at my office to tell me, "Kyle went home."

I considered how God heals us either in heaven or on earth, and this time He chose to take Kyle to heaven and give him a new body. "He's in heaven now," I said, and a few moments of silence followed.

"No," Renee said, "he's at home with his mother and playing just like any normal kid."

She went on to explain that the day after our prayer meeting, Kyle was again tested to measure the cancer's progress. They found no cancer cells—not one. With no medical rationale for the change in his condition, the doctors discharged Kyle just days or weeks before his anticipated death. God had healed him.

Another night, I was called to pray for a man named David Lambert. A respiratory therapist, David contracted an infection caused by a rare type of bacteria, group A strep, from a little girl he was treating at Oakland's Children's Hospital. Most die from the disease. By the time I entered his hospital room, gangrene had already set within all of his limbs, turning them black two to three inches below his knees and elbows.

That night, I prayed as intensely as I had with Kyle, wanting desperately to see God restore those black limbs to a healthy flesh color. David's wife, JoEllen, came into the room and asked me if she should give permission for the surgeons to amputate all of David's limbs. Time was of the essence. If they amputated soon, they could probably save David's joints. Otherwise, he could in no way be fitted with prosthetics—that is, if he even survived.

I told her that I felt God wanted to save David's life, but as yet there was no evidence of a miraculous healing. So the doctors amputated all of David's limbs. After months in recovery, David returned home. He had to be carried up and down the steps and had no ability to do anything on his own.

As I was leaving his house one day, JoEllen stopped me, her nine-year-old daughter by her side. She looked me square in the face and asked, "Randy, can you explain to my daughter why God didn't heal her daddy?"

An invisible knife pierced my soul. "No, I cannot," I answered. "In time, God will have to answer that Himself, to you and you alone."

Months later, David recovered enough to be fitted with prosthetics. The sadness continued as this loving family struggled with the challenges of disability.

One day, after leaving their house, JoEllen once again stopped me and said, "God answered my question, Randy."

I waited for the answer.

"The miracle was that He saved my husband. Most die from the fatal type of staph that infected him. *That* was my miracle."

David lived several years after that. They were hard years. We became good friends, and though I would like to report that all ended well, as is often the case in this fallen world, there were numerous trials and suffering. After David died suddenly while eating a burrito, he received his healing, and I envision him in heaven with four strong limbs.

God's Presence Is Powerful

In my ministry I have witnessed hundreds of miraculous healings and hundreds of people who continued to suffer. To this day, I do not know why God heals some and not others. When I ask God why, He tells me that I could not possibly understand. As a two-year-old, I did not understand physics any more than as a man I can understand all of God's ways. But I do understand that His way is always better than mine (see Isaiah 55:8–9). God's creation was perfect, untainted by sickness, discord, death and decay.

Long ago, an act of rebellion against God set forth a continuous erosion of that perfection down through thousands of years and continuing in our day. God's way often became obscured through the effects of human sin. In place of God's original intent within the Garden of Eden, which was to enjoy direct, intimate relationship with His children, God created a patchwork of solutions to bridge the gap between Himself and rebellious humankind—that is, until Jesus Christ's sacrifice eliminated all barriers between us once and for all time.

We humans live predominately isolated lives. No one can fully understand our thoughts, our emotions, our memories or our experiences—except God. There is now no divide between God and His children because Jesus is our "mediator" (1 Timothy 2:5). We can talk to Jesus as if talking with a best friend. And being separated from Jesus feels like losing a best friend. That God knows all and even cares enough about us to know the number of hairs on our heads (see Luke 12:7) should fill us with assurance beyond circumstances, especially when trials appear insurmountable.

I know you might not feel that way in times of suffering and death. Since my time with Jesus, I have never doubted God's reality, or His love, but it still grieves me to experience the separation of loved ones at death. The great chasm between heaven and this world explained in Luke 16:26 prevents those in heaven from being reminded of the sadness they experienced on earth. There is only joy in heaven, and no tribulation can sully that joy for our loved ones in heaven, which explains why we will have to wait to see our deceased loved ones again, because in our world there is suffering.

For one brief moment in time, God bridged that chasm for me at the death of my father. I admired my father immensely. He was a strong World War II hero and former football player whose love spoke in actions more than words. At 85 years of age, he and my mother moved to be closer to my family in San Diego. The day before moving into their new home, my father tripped and broke his jawbone on a table in our home, which caused cerebral hemorrhaging as an artery in his brain burst.

About a week later, my father lay in bed with no ability to communicate with us, struggling for each breath. As death approached, I sat beside him, whispering Scripture verses and God's promises into his ear. The Holy Spirit instructed me to encourage my father and ease his passage.

A beautiful fragrance flooded my nostrils. (Most of the time I cannot smell anything because of sinus congestion and blocked nasal passageways. But in that moment, I smelled perfectly the sweet perfume of flowers with an aroma more beautiful than anything I had smelled before.) I turned and asked my mother about her perfume or hairspray—she wore none. No one and nothing in that room bore any artificial scent. I smelled the presence of God much as I had smelled it with Jesus in heaven.

During my father's final stages of dying, my mother, my wife, my sister, my niece, a nurse and I joined hands in a circle around my father's bed as we prayed the Lord's Prayer together. At the echo of our amen, my father stopped breathing and went to heaven.

Later, as I asked God about the sweet perfume, He led me to the Song of Solomon in the Bible, where the Shulamite woman declared that God's love is better than wine: "Because of the fragrance of your good ointments, your name is ointment poured forth" (Song of Solomon 1:3–4 NKJV). When I spoke assurances to my father as he died, the Holy Spirit ushered me into a secret place in which I could smell that anointed ointment that was poured forth—the fragrance of God.

I had prayed with my father years before as he gave his life to Jesus Christ. Second Corinthians 2:15 says, "For we are to God the pleasing aroma of Christ among those who are being saved and those who are perishing." I thank God that He gave me that gift of His presence and of the salvation and perishing aroma of my father, all in that one beautiful scent, as a signifier of my father's ascent to heaven.

I almost beat my father to heaven, but now he will be there to welcome me. And I fully expect to smell God's fragrance at the end just as I did when I met Jesus in heaven at the cusp of my own death. There is nothing like the sweet fragrance of God; and there is nothing like the sweet fragrance of God's children to him. I call both the fragrances of Love. What does this have to do with receiving power from God? There is power in His presence.

I remember being at a Chicago dinner event in the mid-1980s. After our salads were served, Jim Thompson, who was governor of Illinois at the time, introduced former-President Ronald Reagan. The band played "Hail to the Chief" as Reagan walked toward the microphone. His presence spoke power and prestige. I was in awe being within several feet of the most powerful leader in the world.

How much greater is the powerful impact of the King of kings and Lord of lords? Now consider this: As Christ followers, we take that power wherever we go because we are "temples of the Holy Spirit" (1 Corinthians 6:19). The same power that raised Jesus from the grave is within you.

The coming of the Holy Spirit on the Day of Pentecost brought a great outpouring of the presence of God. And God is present with you and each of His children now through the Holy Spirit. He is present in fellowship with other believers (see Matthew 18:20). He is present in your heart. And this gives you power to triumph over anything.

The fruit of the Holy Spirit includes joy. So even though Satan is "the accuser" of the saints (Revelation 12:10), "we overwhelmingly conquer through Him who loved us" (Romans 8:37 NASB). The "joy of the LORD" is a source of great strength for us in the most difficult trials of life (Nehemiah 8:10).

God gives us a choice: We can focus either on the things of this earth, which are influenced by the devil, or on the things above. Satan and his minions wreak havoc, whereas God's Spirit causes peace. We can dwell on the things that cause us anxiety or on the things that are true, honorable, right, pure, lovely and of good repute (see Philippians 4:6–8). In other words, as believers, we have the choice to rejoice, and we must deliberately exercise that choice through our relationship with God. And we must fight against the powers and principalities that try to destroy our joy.

God Has Power over the Enemy

We do not live in a spiritual vacuum. Revelation 5:11 tells us that there are "myriads of myriads, and thousands of thousands" of angels (NASB). The Greek word for "myriads" (Deuteronomy 33:2; Daniel 7:9–10; Hebrews 12:22; Revelation 5:11) can be translated "ten thousand times ten thousand."[1] So myriads of myriads means there are more than a hundred million angels.[2] That is about the population of the five largest cities in the world combined.[3]

Angels are spirit beings without physical bodies, though they still have personalities (see also Hebrews 1:7, 14).[4] About a third of the heavenly angels sided with Satan and were cast out of heaven to the earth (see Revelation 12:4). The Bible teaches that fallen angels are invisible spirits created by God. Satan employs them as his agents of wickedness. The Bible calls them demons, fallen angels, devils, and unclean spirits. Demons can inflict disease, ruining bodies and souls (see Luke 9:42).

Satan and his demons cannot possess Christians because the Holy Spirit indwells and protects us (see 1 John 4:4), yet these demons can possess unbelievers and oppress believers. Although demons can oppress people and tempt them to sin, they cannot make people choose sin. Demons fear God's presence (see James 2:19) and cannot rob people of their free will. The demons can whisper lies and confusion and make deceptive suggestions all aimed at denying God His desire for "all people to be saved and to come to a knowledge of the truth" (1 Timothy 2:4).

Most people would rather talk about heaven than hell and hear about angels while ignoring demons. God wants us to know about hell and about demons. The Bible references hell even more than it does heaven, perhaps because we are more inclined to accept the evidence of heaven than the evidence of hell. Heaven is more pleasant.

The good news is that when you welcome God's presence through prayer, the Spirit of Jesus Christ takes authority over all. What is more, God gives you that same power through His Son. Jesus gave the apostles the authority to bind and loose (speak and act under God's authority) as the foundational representatives for the Church. The apostles did not act arbitrarily nor operate apart from the Holy Spirit (see Acts 2:42–47; 4:28–33). God ordained them and us as spiritual warriors.

Paul's deliverance of the slave girl in Acts 16:18 testifies of our empowerment to take authority over demons: "And this she kept doing for many days. Paul, having become greatly annoyed, turned and said to the spirit, 'I command you in the name of Jesus Christ to come out of her.' And it came out that very hour" (ESV). In the same verse in the NIV, Paul rebuked the spirit: "In the name of Jesus Christ I command you to come out of her!" Paul's words bound (restricted or restrained) the evil spirit's influence as it pertained to the slave girl. That same power and authority that Paul exercised has been given to all Christians.

On many occasions I have been asked to pray for people experiencing demonic oppression and possession. Most of the time when I walked into a demonic situation, it was like entering a room full of drunken gang members while being surrounded and protected by eight-foot giants empowered by God almighty—no contest. I just said something to the angels like, "Have at it, guys," and the gang members scurried away like mice after hearing a 25-pound cat growl.

One distinct example during my ascent to heaven as I lay dying in the hospital might help to explain the power of Jesus Christ's authority. I previously mentioned some battling figures as I ascended to heaven. These may have been a vision of "the spiritual forces of evil in the heavenly realms," as referenced in Ephesians 6:12. I distinctly recall two sides fighting each other. In the distance were rolling hills with a middle ground that appeared parched. On the one side were ghastly-looking giants using tarnished weapons like spears. On the other side equally gargantuan figures used brilliantly glistening swords. All of the figures appeared muscular with pronounced features, like large heads and long arms, though I could not distinguish their exact appearance from a distance. I did not see any figures on the ground; however, I did notice that some of the figures appeared weary, while others fought robustly.

As bizarre as that seems to me now, at the time I could sense an immense battle, either for my soul or for the souls of others. All I know is that upon my ascension, with no idea as to where I was going, there was a power I could source, and His name was Jesus Christ. This gave me an assurance that all was well with my soul. I kept calling out His name, and what followed was peace. And ultimately, my time with Jesus in heaven. That vision during my ascent taught me this lesson: There is power in the mere mention of Jesus Christ. Victory arises through declaring Christ's authority in the heavenly realms.

I will give you another example of how this power is relevant today. One evening the pastor of our church called and asked me to visit the home of a family whose ten-year-old son had been experiencing nightmares. These were not just your average nightmares. The boy started hearing voices and seeing vapory figures while awake. Not a night went by without these harrowing nightmares and visages causing the boy to wake up screaming. This had lasted for well over a year, and the boy's health had begun to deteriorate.

When I entered the boy's room with his parents, I could sense the demonic oppression in the room. It pressed against my soul as though someone had informed me of some terrible news—an intuition that felt heavy in the boy's dark room. Hours before, I had been praying before entering the room. Upon sensing the oppressive demons, I started praying what I call a "warrior's prayer." Warriors do not petition their enemies to leave; they demand it. And if the enemy does not leave, they release their mightiest weapon against the enemy—in this case, the authority of God over demons (see Luke 10:17).

I asked the older sister to take her brother to another room. Next, I looked for any evidence of something the demons may have grabbed onto as a hook for oppressing this little boy. Some gruesome comic books lay on a table, and what appeared to be an inverted cross had been chalked over the wall. "Get me some soap and water so we can wipe this off," I instructed the parents. Once we discarded the comic books and erased the upside-down cross, I very simply and with the utmost conviction declared God's authority over the room and the boy and the entire household:

"In the name of Jesus Christ, I demand that you leave this place, and I commit this family into the loving hands of Yahweh [the sacred Hebrew name of God] as I plead the blood of Jesus Christ over this family and this place." There was no doubt in my mind that God would answer my prayers and take control. Father God was in charge.

Peace instantly flooded that room. I sensed joy instead of oppression. I even felt like singing a song of worship but knew that I needed to pray with the boy and his family first. We all met in the living room, and all the family members gave their lives to Christ, with each asking forgiveness and inviting God to take full control of their lives. The boy's countenance changed. He smiled like any liberated little boy should smile.

Then we returned to his room. I left a children's Bible on his nightstand where the comics once lay and instructed him to read it every day and to not read any more of those demonic comics. Like any warrior, I discarded the weapons of the enemy.

"How do you feel being in this room now?" I asked the boy.

"Can God send His angels to be with me?" he answered.

"Surely, He can and probably already has sent angels to protect you."

"Oh, that makes sense," he said, "because I think Jesus said that He's put one in my room."

Months later, I asked the parents and the boy if he had experienced any more night terrors. "No," they all answered. In fact, the family was so "on fire" for God that they started a Bible study in their home. Joy had replaced sadness and dissention in that family. That boy would later be a leader in the children's classroom at church. And though of course they were not a jolly family all of the time, they always knew where to go when troubles surfaced—to the cross of Jesus Christ.

Coming to the cross is not just a theological statement. It means keeping the cross of Christ central so that the power of God can protect us from the forces of false teachings and evil influences. First Peter 2:24–25 says:

> "[Jesus] himself bore our sins" in his body on the cross, so that we might die to sins and live for righteousness; "by his wounds you have been healed." For "you were like sheep going astray," but now you have returned to the Shepherd and Overseer of your souls.

That is the power of God, which can be manifested through us to combat every evil influence in our lives.

I have witnessed the deliverance of people possessed with demons, and I can tell you that it in no way resembles the Hollywood horror-movie version. Most of the time, God instantly frees the person. Sometimes their heads jerk back and they begin convulsing as the enemy fights back and tries to frighten me or others around me. I admit that, at first, these manifestations frightened me, but now they just appear to me like silly grown-ups showing up in Halloween costumes and saying, "Boo."

Demons are fools. Why else would they join a rebellious angel (Satan) who had been created by God? They were foolish enough to think Satan could give them something better than God almighty, who had created them all. If one or more demons try to oppress you or your loved ones with impressions of doom and gloom, then assert your right as a child of Jesus Christ and command them to leave. Remember, you have the victory in Christ.

God Wants to Liberate You

All too often, influences beyond our comprehension steal our joy. These powers may be a demonic voice saying, *God can't forgive you because your sin is too terrible*, or a false teaching such as, *God is watching over you, ready to pounce on you the moment you do something bad.* Both keep us from the freedom of being in the presence of the Holy Spirit. That is why I am sharing this important lesson about the powers and principalities of this world.

God is ready to forgive anyone (see Acts 3:19; Daniel 9:9; 1 John 1:9; Psalm 103:12; Matthew 26:28). He is merciful and patient (see Psalm 145:8; 2 Samuel 24:14; Luke 6:36). Do not accept the false teaching that God was different in nature in the Old Testament from the New Testament, like some Dr. Jekyll and Mr. Hyde character. There are more references to mercy in the Old Testament than in the New Testament. God has always been merciful. God has never changed.

No one can operate in the freedom of Jesus Christ until he or she understands how great the love of our Father God is to all His beloved children. He does not want to condemn you—He wants to liberate you. Hebrews 13:5 quotes Moses' words in Deuteronomy 31:6: "The Lord . . . will never leave you nor forsake you." Indeed, "if we confess our sins, he is faithful and just and will forgive us our sins and purify us from all unrighteousness" (1 John 1:9), and "everyone who calls on the name of the Lord will be saved" (Romans 10:13).

Salvation is not a license to sin; rather, it is an indwelling of God's Spirit that gives us the power to become more like Christ. The walk in Christ conforms us to Jesus Christ, which causes us to not desire sin by transforming our desire to love God more than anything else. Earnestly desiring to know God more and to spend more time with Him ushers us into God's presence. Simply put, the more time we spend with God, the more like Him we will become and the more we will rise (not fall) in love with God.

Like a household that receives its power from high-voltage transmission lines, so we must receive our power from the source of absolute power, Father God. When we depend on our own strength, we lose our greatest source of power—the Creator of heaven, earth and the entire universe. Being filled with the power of God frees us from fear and the demonic influences that cause fear. The Holy Spirit heals us and transforms us. He also transmits that power through us to heal and edify others. That is the power of God!

—7—

Dying to Self

Charlie Wedemeyer was a good-looking star quarterback for the Punahou School in Hawaii who also played for the revered Michigan State University football team. He married his beautiful high school sweetheart, Lucy. After graduating with a master's degree, Charlie got a prime position coaching Los Gatos High School football in the San Francisco Bay Area. Life was good. Then Charlie was diagnosed with Lou Gehrig's disease. He noticed the first sign of the disease in 1976 when he began having trouble pressing the chalk against a blackboard as he taught math classes. He continued to coach as long as possible, until he could no longer speak. Lucy would communicate for him by watching his eyes twitch.

Renee and I attended a Christian marriage conference at which Charlie and Lucy spoke; actually, Lucy interpreted Charlie's eye twitches in full sentences. I recall looking at Renee and saying, "No way is his wife giving a full speech interpretation from Charlie just by watching his eye movements."

A few years later we met Charlie and Lucy at a family retreat for the disabled hosted by Joni Eareckson Tada. By this time, Charlie was completely confined to a gurney and required constant medical attention. We were impressed with Charlie's love for Jesus as he testified of God's amazing grace through Lucy.

About a year later, Renee and I were working at the Billy Graham Crusades in the San Jose sports arena. As Charlie was being wheeled down the stadium hallway, accompanied by Lucy and his medical team, I told him, "You inspire me." The medical attendants halted Charlie's gurney so we could communicate. His eyes started twitching, and Lucy provided an interpretation: Charlie was very touched that his life had affected me so much. Through Lucy, Charlie asked about me. I answered. Lucy interpreted his responses. Then something amazing happened.

I asked Lucy to stop interpreting Charlie's sentences to me because I felt as though I understood Charlie without Lucy's translation. As Charlie's eyes twitched, I began speaking in full sentences what I understood he had communicated. When I asked Lucy to confirm, she said, "Yes, that's absolutely what he said."

Next, I asked Charlie if I was accurate with my interpretations. Charlie's eyes twitched once for yes, confirming that I understood his expressions. We carried on a full conversation for about twenty minutes with just the twitching of Charlie's eyes and my spoken words. Now, I am not trained in the language of "eye twitching," but I am trained in the language of the Holy Spirit.

That is how God speaks to our hearts—not just with words, but most profoundly through a "sense of knowing" that derives God's meaning from connection with His Spirit. And the way I communicate with God these days is different from the way I heard and felt Jesus in heaven.

If you are familiar with *Star Trek*, you may recall the Vulcan mind meld. (Yes, I am a sort of Trekkie, so please bear with me as I use this analogy.) The mind meld was a telepathic link between two individuals that allowed for an intimate exchange of thought, enabling them to share their consciousness as a kind of gestalt. Spock used it to communicate with Vulcans and humans. Oddly enough, the way we communicate with the Holy Spirit is similar in some respects, only the connection is Spirit to spirit, not mind to mind. The way I communicated with Charlie was on a spiritual level, with the Holy Spirit as our interpreter.

Not long after my meeting with Charlie at the crusade, I read the news that he had died at the age of 64. Charlie had given his all to Jesus. He had sacrificed everything to God. Charlie taught me that when we are willing to give God our all, He gives us the strength to triumph over any loss by exchanging our loss for a more profound purpose. Charlie exuded more joy than most able-bodied persons I know. I perceived it on his face and in his spirit, and that happened because Charlie carried his cross for God.

Now, chances are God will not allow you to suffer like Charlie, but if He does allow something to be taken from you, it is because He wants to give you something greater in return. You will get to know Him better. You will develop more intimacy with God through your loss. And your purpose will be greater than ever before. I did not spend much time with Charlie and Lucy, but they made more of a positive impact on my life (and countless others') than 99 percent of the people I have met.

Finding Satisfaction in Jesus

My favorite spot on earth overlooks the Pacific Ocean. It is the closest place to heaven's peace that I can find on earth. I often sit on a rock jutting over a ragged cliff to view the disappearing ocean in the distance and the tide washing across the sand below. When the waters recede, they leave behind glistening pebbles kissed by the sun. Then I look over the glassy spectacle of the vast ocean in contrast to the swelling waves about to crash over the beach and the soothing sounds of pounding waves thereafter. The wonder of how something so calming can come crashing down to reveal its hidden treasures to me represents the ebb and flow of life.

A superficial glimpse of our life may appear smooth to the common observer, but when something pushes against us, like the wind pressing against still waters, our peace can come crashing down. When the source of disturbance recedes, what is left behind represents the afterglow from God's light turning that crashing blow into a soothing sense of something redeemed. God appears to shine His light over our troubles just as the sun shines its light over the rocky residue of the ocean's receding waves. Returning that which was lost for a greater gain is at the heart of God's plan for you and me.

In Matthew 16:24 Jesus said, "If any of you wants to be my follower, you must give up your own way, take up your cross, and follow me" (NLT). That verse confounded me for a long time. I used to think this meant we needed to sacrifice the pleasures of life for some monastic vow or endure sickness, the loss of a job, etc. Now I have come to understand that carrying "your own cross" means being willing to sacrifice all to God (Luke 14:27 NLT).

That afterglow from our trials is God revealing the stepping-stones to our grander purpose. Enduring the "crushing waves" that cause disruptions in our life is part of carrying our cross for Christ. This also represents the conundrum of why each of us must endure the harshness in this world when life's pressures come crashing down on us.

If you wonder if you are ready to take up your cross, consider whether you would be willing to alienate a family member by sharing your faith or to give up a bad habit that gives you an addictive pleasure or to leave your job for a higher calling if God says go. If a terrorist held a gun to your head and told you to deny Jesus Christ or die, would you be willing to lose your life?

Taking up your cross and following Jesus means being willing to surrender all in order to follow Him, which does not mean that we will face these tests or be called to do these things; it means that in our hearts, we must be *willing* to do them. This is called "dying to self."

There are actually two facets of dying to self: (1) the old self dies and (2) the new self comes to life (see John 3:3–7). But we believers are "born again" not only when we find salvation (verse 3)—we continue dying to self as part of the process of being set apart to fulfill our special purpose in being conformed to the image of Jesus Christ. As such, dying to self is both a one-time event and a lifelong process.

That process is a call to absolute submission in trusting that Father God knows best. Jesus said this about sacrifice: "Whoever wants to save his life will lose it, but whoever loses his life because of Me will save it. What is a man benefited if he gains the whole world, yet loses or forfeits himself?" (Luke 9:25–26 HCSB). That is a tough calling, one that requires some sincere soul searching.

Could you endure anything for God? Before answering yes, consider that Peter felt the same way yet denied Jesus after the Roman soldiers arrested Him. At the cross, all the disciples deserted Jesus and fled. True allegiance to Christ is tested not in words but in the moments that define our character.

During my near-death experience, I experienced the joy of heaven, which to me seemed better than any treasure trove in this world. Nothing in this world can satisfy one iota as much as our relationship with Christ. And being willing to give God our all is absolutely worth it. No sincere believer wants a part-time relationship with God. Instead, we desire the fullness of everything God desires for us, and He in turn wants our all.

If, however, we pride ourselves in terms of worldly success and are unwilling to sacrifice that status for the sake of God, then we may lose our greatest treasures in heaven (see Matthew 6:19–21). If we decide to embrace an unhealthy relationship, our relationship with God will suffer. If we want a part-time devotional life with God, we will fail to live life to its fullness as God intended.

How many times have you striven after success only to find it entirely elusive or disappointing? For me, I have had the nice house, fine car, promotions and status, but they never fully satisfied me. It is almost cliché that people who have "everything in the world" oftentimes lack joy. Please know that I am not espousing a vow of poverty. Quite the contrary, God desires to "give good gifts" to His children (Matthew 7:11), but only if we ask for those gifts in alignment with His purpose. Only my devotion to God and loving others has fed my soul. That is the "bread of life" (John 6:5; see also vv. 32–34), the spiritual "meat" described in Hebrews 5:12–14 (KJV). Everything else amounts to just empty calories.

More to the point, relationships have defined the most important elements of my life—first, my relationship with Christ, and then my relationships with others. When something jeopardized my relationship with God or hindered my Kingdom purpose, I am thankful God removed that "cancer."

Sacrificing our lives to God means giving our Lord absolute authority to eliminate everything that gets between God and us, so we can love God with our whole heart, soul and mind (see Matthew 22:36–37). "This is the first and greatest commandment," Jesus declared in verse 38. The second is similar: love others with as much devotion as we love ourselves (see verses 39–40).

Hey, I do not know about you, but I have struggled with sacrificing my all to God so that I might love Him with all my heart, soul and mind. The cares of this world keep getting in the way. The human body and our moral and physical frailties tend to override our willingness to do what is right (see

Matthew 26:41), especially when we are fatigued or consumed with worldly responsibilities. And as for loving my neighbor as much as I love myself? Well, sometimes when my neighbor takes my parking spot or commits some other offense, I am certainly not caring about that neighbor's needs as much as mine.

So did Jesus establish a commandment we cannot keep? Yes and no. By ourselves, we cannot keep this commandment any more than we could have kept the Ten Commandments God gave to Moses on Mount Sinai. And yet God does not set us up for failure. If He gives us a commandment, He also gives us the way to keep it. God established that "way," as Jesus described in John 14:6: "I am the way and the truth and the life. No one comes to the Father except through me." The way to the Father is through Jesus Christ. The indwelling of Christ's Spirit is what enables us to love God and one another—that same Spirit who produces genuine love in our hearts.

Relationship lies at the core of loving God and our neighbors. God esteems relationship so much that His Word, the Bible, contains thousands of passages that teach us how to deepen, protect and enjoy our relationships with Him and the people He has placed in our lives. Relationships of love matter most—especially getting closer to God, immersing ourselves in His presence, steeping ourselves in His Word and asking the Holy Spirit to take full control regardless of the consequences.

"The way," as Jesus described Himself in John 14:6, represents both His name and a way of life, both His Person and a set of actions, for all believers. By dwelling with Jesus and following Him, we find abundant life. In a sense, Jesus is the internal GPS (Global Positioning System), or rather "Kingdom Positioning System," for our soul. But His way is not an easy way, "because narrow is the gate and difficult is the way which leads to life, and there are few who find it" (Matthew 7:14 NKJV). It is, however, the only path that leads to intimacy with God and each other.

That intimacy to me represents the soothing waters of my soul and a comforting voice to my spirit. When God's way becomes our way, we can discover a little bit of heaven on earth. Heaven is a place, true, but Jesus is the way toward everything that is good in this life.

My Mother's Peaceful Passing

As I mentioned at the beginning of this book, my mother suffered from Alzheimer's, a disease that robs its victims of the capacity to think clearly. She spoke randomly with no coherence of thoughtful expression. Yet when I saw her or heard her voice, she was still Mom. Her essence never faded. That is because her soul remained intact even though her mind was diseased.

Likewise, when we followers of Christ lose our way through sin or by following the ways of this world instead of Christ's way, we become disoriented, lacking any true joy. Even so, Jesus remains at the core of who we are, and we need only follow His directions to reestablish our true pathway in Christ.

I witnessed that profoundly at my mother's passing. One day in the fall of 2018, the Holy Spirit impressed upon my spirit a knowledge that my mother did not have long to live. He also promised me that He would prolong her life so I could say my final good-bye and also give her a clear mind so she would know me.

Within 48 hours of receiving this word, I hopped on a flight from San Diego to Moline, Illinois, and drove 46 miles to her skilled-care facility in Galesburg, Illinois. Upon entering her room, I beheld the gaunt figure of my mother, once beautiful and loving, as she slept.

Then I sat on her bed, held her hand and whispered in her ear, "Mom, I'm here. This is your son, Randy. God has you in His embrace now."

She opened her eyes and said, "Randy."

Since she had slipped into the latter stages of Alzheimer's, I had not heard my mother say my name. But in that moment, she looked into my eyes and smiled, gripping me tightly.

For three days, our spirits communed with each other in the language of love beyond the scope of any trivial words. There was a deep understanding of the close bond between us as interpreted by the Holy Spirit, a sense of knowing, a feeling of peace, an assurance of caring—love born from the soul.

On her final day, my mom's bright azure-blue eyes turned a darker shade of midnight blue. Her once intense stare softened as she seemed to drift to a distant place. Her grip tightened. I knew then that my mother was more in heaven than on earth.

God's Spirit told me it was time.

I bent over, spoke the Lord's Prayer and sang "Amazing Grace" into my mother's ear while thinking of the sweet lullabies she once whispered in my ear when I was a child. I remembered my time with Jesus as I neared death and He held my hand. Then a vision of Jesus outstretching His hand to my mother appeared clearly to me.

"Mom," I said, "you can let go of my hand now because Jesus will take yours from this time and forever, and I will see you soon."

She let go of my hand and breathed her final breath.

My mother is free today. Her mind is clear and her body is strong, and all the while her spirit never changed. She is in heaven with many of my loved ones.

I am so blessed that God gave me a final opportunity to be with my mom and to communicate with her spiritually and with love. I now have peace. God is good even through the tears.

Rejoicing in God

For a while I worked at the Christ-centered organization Teen Challenge, one of the most successful rehabilitation programs on record, confirmed by independent studies by researchers at Northwestern University[1] and the Association of Christian Alcohol & Drug Counselors.[2] Those in treatment find little trouble surrendering to the higher power of Jesus Christ because they have already surrendered to a much lower power.

One night I conducted a Bible study in one of the Teen Challenge homes in the Chicago area. All participants were believers, and most of them studied Scripture multiple times throughout the day. I found myself scrambling for a verse to complete the study. Former gang members with tattoos signifying their number of kills leafed through their highlighted Bibles like children opening their first Christmas present. No one in the room could find it either.

Suddenly, the oakwood doors separating the living room from the study room burst open. A boy with Down syndrome had rushed downstairs from his bedroom, through the living room and into our gathering. "God told me to give you a verse," he said. It was the exact verse for which we had been diligently searching for over ten minutes.

How did this mentally disabled teen know the verse and feel compelled to give it to us without participating in our study? It was because this young man's mind was surrendered to God. That is how we need to be with God. Let go and let God have His way with us. Intimacy with God is paramount. He has done His part; now we need to will our mind, body and soul to God. And that, friends, is how we can hear the voice of God. That teen bypassed his damaged brain to find God in his most sacred place, and that is where he heard God.

God so desired to be intimately involved with His children that He created a habitation for us, Spirit to spirit within our inner sanctum. Throughout all of history, God has found a way to dwell in the midst of His children despite the physical, mental or emotional obstacles that have impeded our relationships. Because He loves us so very much, God has always established a dwelling place amid His people or "pitched His tent" with us, so to speak—first in the tabernacle as explained in Exodus 36:8–39:43 and later in the Old Testament period within the temple—"that we might know Him, love Him, enjoy Him, and glorify Him *coram Deo*, before His face, now and forever." [3]

In John 1:14, the word *logos*, referring to Jesus, is paired with *skēnoō*, "dwelt," which literally means "tabernacled" with us.[4] God dwelled (literally "fellowshiped") among His people in the Person of His Son, the Lord Jesus Christ. Now, in this age of grace, the Spirit of God dwells within each believer and among us (see 1 Corinthians 3:16). God has always given us the way to His presence. How could God, the One who loves us more than anyone else, not want to be with His beloved? Let's take a look at the exceptional effort God made to be present with His believers, beginning with the dedication of His first temple in 827 BC.

God Inhabits His Temple

The Jerusalem temple was completed under the direction of King Solomon after seven years of construction. It housed the Ark of the Covenant after a seven-day celebration welcoming the manifestation of God's divine presence. Then a curtain was hung to restrict entrance in the holiest of holy places, wherein the Spirit of God dwelled. The holy room could be entered only by the High Priest on the Day of Atonement (Yom Kippur) after sanctifying himself. This was the way in which God communicated with His people, through the prophets and the High Priest. It may not have been the ideal way of fellowshiping with His children as God originally enjoyed with Adam and Eve, but it was nevertheless the best way for God to maintain relationship in that ancient fallen world.

As unfortunately often happens with humans, God's children, the Jews, rebelled against God and His way. After

Solomon's death, the kings of the kingdom of Israel practiced idolatry. God sent prophets repeatedly to admonish the Jews, but they refused to change their ways. Worshiping idols was devotion to the things of this world rather than devotion to God (just as it is today).

Thus, the temple Solomon built was destroyed in 587–586 BC by Nebuchadnezzar, the king of Babylon. The Bible book 2 Kings describes the final days: "In the fifth month, . . . Nebuzaradan, the captain of the bodyguard, a servant of the king of Babylon, came to Jerusalem. He burned the house of the Lord, the king's house, and all the houses of Jerusalem; every great house he burned down" (2 Kings 25:8–9 NRSV). The Jews were then enslaved by the Babylonians. Having forsaken their first love, the Jews had abandoned God's protective covering by ignoring His presence.

This event marked a turning point in history because it marked the end of the Judean state and a departure of God's presence. God revealed His sorrow in Jeremiah 8:18–9:3. And yes, God has feelings. Speaking of the Jews' failures, God said in Hosea 11:8: "My heart is changed within me; all my compassion is aroused." The New Testament further expresses God's emotions in Ephesians 4:30: "And do not grieve the Holy Spirit of God, with whom you were sealed for the day of redemption." In this verse, the word for "grieve" is from the Greek word *lypeō*, which means a pain or grief that can only be experienced between two people who deeply love each other.[5] God's emotions are always righteous and always from a point of deep love. He never stops loving His children, but the Jews stopped loving Him.

The Jews had lost their way. After witnessing the slaughter and judgment in the spiritual realms that caused the temple to be destroyed, Ezekiel cried out, "Ah, Lord GOD! Will you make a full end of the remnant of Israel?" (Ezekiel 11:13 ESV). In verse 17, God responded by promising that He would bring the Jews back to the land and put a "new spirit" in them (verse 19). Most understood at the time that the final restoration of the Jews would take place in the last days, the end times, when Israel would finally receive her Messiah, when the way of God would align itself with the ways of His chosen people (see Ezekiel chapters 36–48).

Eventually, the kingdom of Persia defeated Babylon around 538 BC. After the Jews started seeking after God, King Cyrus of Persia allowed the Jews to return to Jerusalem to rebuild the temple destroyed by the Babylonians. Most scholars date the completion of the restored temple to 516–515 BC when Nehemiah led the rebuilding of Jerusalem after its destruction by Nebuchadnezzar 152 years prior.[6] Nehemiah spent days and nights reading God's Word with the Jews, immersing them in God's presence until they started weeping in repentance. "The joy of the Lord is your strength," he told them (Nehemiah 8:10). Hence, the people began "rejoicing" (verse 12).

Their joy resulted from the spiritual strength they gained by being in God's presence, steeping in His Word. Rejoicing and being glad in the Lord can be found throughout the Bible (see Psalms 5:11; 9:2; 32:11; 33:1; 40:16). And this joy is not based on emotions or born out of circumstances, as Paul testified more than once in the New Testament. He said God's servants are "sorrowful, yet always rejoicing" (2 Corinthians 6:10) and exhorted the believers in Philippi to "rejoice in the Lord" (Philippians 3:1; 4:4). Paul and Nehemiah found their joy in intimate relationship with God after soaking themselves in His presence. That was as true then as it is today.

I would hazard to guess that God's most earnest desire is to be close to us. Why else would He create us in His image to have fellowship and then sacrifice Himself to establish closeness? Even if you consider yourself unworthy, Jesus found you worthy of Himself. Try letting go. God speaks profoundly to those whose mind is surrendered to His Spirit.

Glimpses of God's Love

The smell of funeral flowers played in my mind as I lay in the emergency room bed. I imagined how my memorial service would play out. Who would come to the service? Would they play my favorite songs? I envisioned meeting Jesus again, only this time I considered everything I had done and not done in my life. This mental playback was not unlike my near-death experience about two years prior when I saw a flashback of my life while ascending from my body before meeting Jesus.

Friends, this was the experience from my *second* series of blood clots that occurred about two years after my NDE. After facing death, and heaven, the possibility of finally dying seemed almost anticlimactic. That is because on earth we face only glimpses of God's love, but in heaven that love is fully manifested. This time in the ER, however, my clots were treated before advancing to a critical point. Facing the possibility of death on this occasion did not result in trepidation; rather, it elicited thoughts of God's love.

Being intimate with God always brings joy—not by emotion, but through relationship. The key to unlocking joy is intimate relationship with the One who loves us most. In Psalm 32:11, David wrote, "Be glad in the Lord and rejoice, you righteous ones; and shout for joy, all you who are upright in heart" (NASB). Given David's moral failures (e.g., committing adultery with Bathsheba and murdering her husband), we know that he is not talking about his perfection. Instead, his joy finds its source through the righteousness of God and God's mercy in conferring forgiveness to each repentant believer. Knowing his Lord intimately, David proclaimed in Psalm 86:13, "Great is your love toward me; you have delivered me from the depths, from the realm of the dead."

As it was with David, repentance reestablishes relationship with God by cleansing us of unrighteousness. First Corinthians

3:17 says that "God's temple is sacred" and that we believers are that temple. How then do we keep our temples cleansed? When we accepted Christ, the blood of Christ cleansed us by faith—by taking God at His word. We must also keep our temples clean. So how do we do that? First John 1:9 teaches us how to keep our temple clean: "If we confess our sins, he is faithful and just and will forgive us our sins and purify us from all unrighteousness." Keeping the temple clean starts by asking the Holy Spirit to show us where we are not like Christ and then asking God to forgive us of our wrongdoings.

The Bible not only promises us complete pardon for all of our past transgressions; it also promises God's presence and sustaining grace in the present and the joy of eternity with Him in the future. It tells us that God's power "has granted to us everything pertaining to life and godliness, through the true knowledge of Him who called us by His own glory and excellence" (2 Peter 1:3 NASB) and reveals God as full of joy (see Zephaniah 3:17).

The believers in Nehemiah's time discovered joy simply by being with God and knowing the Father's and the Son's love, rejoicing in God alone. We can find joy in the same way. When steeped in God's presence, we should also be filled with His joy. We can rejoice in calling God our Father and in being able to come boldly into His presence through our adoption in Christ. There is no greater joy than the joy of being with God.

Throughout the course of human history, God has always desired to fellowship with those of us whom He created in His image (see Genesis 1:27). Elohim, the Hebrew name for God, has gone to immeasurable lengths to establish and then reestablish close relationship with His people. He has been incredibly patient in building bridges between Himself and His beloved.

Our forefathers and foremothers, on the other hand, have continually resisted God's way, and we are no different. As the saying goes, "the apple doesn't fall far from the tree." We are the descendants of our forefathers and foremothers, starting with Adam and Eve. Disobedience to God breeds separation from Him, requiring the final act of God's love for His beloved.

That ultimate act of love is described in John 3:16: "For God so loved the world that he gave his one and only Son, that whoever believes in him shall not perish but have eternal life." Despite the twists and turns of obedience and rebellion throughout human history, God found a way to establish lasting and unbreakable relationship with us. He sacrificed His only begotten Son so that His Spirit could reside in us. God no longer places His presence in a man-made creation; He places it in *His* creation. And the only way to inhabiting God's presence is through "the way and the truth and the life," that is, Jesus Christ (John 14:6).

Do you now catch a glimpse of how much God loves you? He's done everything possible to instill the joy of knowing Him completely as your Father, Friend, Comforter, Provider and Protector. He even gave His life for you—*you*. Jesus gave up heaven to live in a fallen, harsh and abusive world so that He could be with you for all of eternity. You are precious in His eyes (see Isaiah 43:4).

If that does not testify of God's love for you, then I ask you: Would you give up heaven for some people destined to torture you and hang you? How much does God absolutely love you? Let's count the ways:

- John 3:16 says He loves you so much that He sacrificed His only Son for you.
- Isaiah 49:16 says He loves you so much that He engraved your name on the palms of His hands.
- Isaiah 54:10 says He loves you so much that His steadfast love will never depart from you.
- Matthew 10:30 says He loves you so much that He numbers the hairs on your head.

- Psalm 147:3 says He loves you so much that He heals your broken heart and wounds.
- Psalm 56:8 says He loves you so much that He collects all your tears in a bottle.
- Jeremiah 31:3 says He loves you so much that His love will be everlasting.
- John 15:14 says He loves you so much that He will consider you a friend just for obeying Him.
- Zephaniah 3:17 says He loves you so much that He delights in you.

Through Christ, we are beloved "children of God" (1 John 3:1). That is absolutely amazing.

Relationship with God is established through belief in and confession of Jesus Christ as the resurrected Son of God (see Romans 10:9). We cannot ever be good enough to earn that relationship. It was a gift from God through Christ. God's holiness required a pathway to atone for the sin that separated a perfect God from an imperfect human race, such that we might be interconnected, then God's love found a way to create intimacy within us.

We consistently underestimate God's love because we too often view love through the prism of our minds. Only through the mind of Christ can we understand God's thoughts (see 1 Corinthians 2:16). We can only grasp the depth and breadth of God's love by drawing close to Him (see Ephesians 3:18).

Consider this: Does not the vastness of the universe speak of His greatness? And yet despite His greatness, God's eyes are upon you. After meeting Jesus, I know that "God is love" (1 John 4:8) and that you are the "apple of his eye" (Deuteronomy 32:10; Zechariah 2:8). That is how I felt, and it is how each of us should feel, whether in heaven or on earth.

Friend, we are broken so we can experience the fullness of God's joy in Him, and Him alone. That brokenness equips us to fulfill our singular purpose in this life. As you experience the process of dying to self, know that God has equipped you to carry your cross through the power of His Holy Spirit. Do not carry the burdens by yourself. Give them to Jesus and He will "give you rest" (Matthew 11:28).

Persevere through your hardships, knowing that God will never leave you. Because you are a believer in Jesus Christ, God's Spirit lives within you. Honor that Spirit with your life. Immerse yourself in the presence of the Spirit of Jesus Christ so you will be "conformed to" His image (Romans 8:29). God has promised you that He will "never leave you nor forsake you" (Hebrews 13:5). You are loved.

Alex's Identity in Jesus

Just after my nephew Alex was diagnosed with schizophrenia and before his brain faded into disease, he wrote several statements of faith, each beginning with, "For this I am certain . . ." Following this declaration, he stated, "I am a child of God," "God loves me," "I will live forever in heaven with Jesus," etc. He filled an entire page with these declarations, knowing that his mind might soon lose its grip on reality. Alex also kept a worn-out Bible and those declarations of his faith by his bedside as a reminder of his true identity. Alex's relationship with Jesus Christ was his anchor, his foundation and his true character.

As the schizophrenia began robbing him of himself, Alex's physical appearance changed dramatically. The once handsome and athletic young man gained over a hundred pounds. His once cheery disposition sometimes turned sour. At the end, Alex needed medicine to restore his rational state of mind. But whenever I prayed with him, I saw through the outer man to the wonderful spirit within him. On the inside, this young man remained "Alex" regardless of his fluctuating emotions and behaviors because Alex's core essence, like my mother's, did not reside in his mind.

Neither does the Holy Spirit reside within our minds or brains. God has tucked His presence inside a holy place walled-off from any outside influence. First Corinthians 6:19 states, "Your body is a temple of the Holy Spirit within you" (ESV). Our bodies are essentially the outer court of that temple. The inner court would be our mind. Finally, an inner sanctum within us is where the Spirit of God dwells, the holy of holies. When Jesus assumes the throne of our life, meaning we became "born again" (John 3:3), our spirit and God's Spirit unite with each other within the inner sanctum. According to 1 Corinthians 6:17, "whoever is united with the Lord is one with him in spirit." Imagine that—we are one with God.

Understanding that the mind does not define our relationship with God proved liberating to me. After all, my own depression seemed at times to separate me from the One who loves me most. Even more troubling was witnessing how my loved ones (such as Annie, my mom and Alex) were transformed into people I could not recognize because their minds took them to an alien place.

Mental illness oftentimes robs people of respect, creates shame and forms a negative image of those who suffer from it. Society tends to judge those who act out their mental illness, even though it is beyond their control. But God does not. He sees the real person behind the mask of a damaged brain, tucked away within the inner sanctum in solitude with His Spirit. That is great consolation to those of us whose minds sometimes play a different role from who we are in Christ. God always finds a way toward intimacy.

Alex died of cardiac arrest one sunny morning in Folsom, California. At 32 he had the body of a seventy-year-old. I gave his eulogy in a packed-out room after a video presentation that showed baby Alex growing into a smiling little boy and then turning into a Leonardo DiCaprio look-alike high school football star.

My eulogy began with a question: "Who was Alex?" He was and is the man I saw behind the mind and body—a loving and devoted follower of Jesus Christ whose spirit shines with love and compassion. That is how God sees His children all the time.

You are beautiful in God's eyes.

—8—

Dying to Meet Jesus

Are you ready to die? Just asking that question may evoke a defensive response, maybe even fear. Maybe your answer is "no way." Maybe it is "beam me up," as the Star Trek character Scotty heard from Captain Kirk before being transported to a foreign galaxy. Whether you are ready or not, that day will come, and it is best to be prepared. So how do you prepare for death? By looking at the other side of it.

Death robs people of reason. It is an unpleasant experience, one that is usually accompanied by pain and loss. When I lost control of my body from a septic infection and blood clots forming throughout my body, I could not think much at all. That is when God took over.

The fantastic news is, Jesus is prepared to intercede on your behalf. He takes over when everything else seems totally out of your control at the cusp of death. The problem remains that too many of us fail to contemplate life in the context of eternity. I would even hazard to guess that most professing Christians question whether their faith is real or imagined. There is that looming doubt that maybe . . . just maybe this Christian belief is just a hope.

Our worldly perspective tends to rob us of our spiritual reality. We are so earthly focused we lose sight of the fact that we are heavenly bound and spiritually made for eternity. We are eternal spirits living in a temporary body. Once in heaven, our life in this world will seem like a "mist" that appeared for a "little while" and then vanished (James 4:14). As believers in Jesus Christ, we do not experience a lifetime in this world; we experience a lifetime in eternity with almost all of it being spent in heaven.

In heaven, only the good will remain. Isaiah 65:16 says, "For the past troubles will be forgotten and hidden from my eyes." In His infinite mercy, God will erase our past troubles, leaving behind thoughts of cherished times. Revelation 21:4 says, "'He will wipe every tear from their eyes. There will be no more death' or mourning or crying or pain, for the old order of things has passed away." We can look forward to that day, but for this day the peaks and valleys within our memory bank serve a profound purpose.

Memories of God's Faithfulness

Our brain reconciles both the good and the bad in this world. Within our memory repository resides a storehouse of experiences that speak afresh of situations and people once remembered. God imbedded within us the means to relive the most important parts of our life to either resolve hurts or encourage us. We remember things faintly that once appeared vividly within our senses at the moment they happened.

Some experiences trigger memories—a classic song, the smell of home-baked cookies, a person who resembles someone from the past. Memories are stored realities. They keep alive people and places and treasured objects. There is a science behind how God created our minds to speak anew, and a reason why memory plays an essential role in our walk with Christ.

During my time researching Alzheimer's as my biopharmaceutical company developed a mechanism of action for combatting this disease, I learned some fascinating facts about the way God designed the brain. He created our brain's "visual processing" center, called the primary visual cortex, located at the back of the brain, which combines signals from our eyes before it stores any details in long-term memory.[1] When we try to remember a situation, our brain chunks together the details, then moves the most influential ones from short- to long-term memory through a selective highway of neurotransmitters. God designed us this way to eliminate unpleasant memories or leave traumatic ones that must be healed, or to assuage our troubled thoughts with comforting images.

Such is the case for my wife, Renee, who recalls vividly to this day a profound event that took place when she was five years old some 47 years ago. Here is how she remembers it:

A calm permeated the dewy October air as the birds cheerfully sang out their tunes. I hopped onto the old rusty red swing in my grandmother's backyard and pushed myself into the air. I listened to the birds cheerfully sing out their songs along with the creaky swing, air pressing over my face and pulling my long hair back, then in reverse with the same thrilling and freeing pull. My feet continued lightly pumping as I looked around me, my eyes drawn to the old oak tree.

Everything stopped as though I was in a still picture and I was in the center of everything. I saw a man standing by the tree and immediately knew it was Jesus. He wore a long white robe with hair longer and wavier than mine. His figure appeared translucent. A warm and welcoming smile appeared on His face as He looked into my eyes. I felt an all-consuming love and peace in that moment, and then He motioned me toward Him. It was not a call for me to run to Him. In my heart I knew

Jesus was beckoning me toward Him. He was saying without words, *Come and have a relationship with me and know that I love you.* Then He disappeared. I remember running into the kitchen and yelling, "Gramma, I just saw Jesus." My gramma just smiled and said, "That's nice, Renee," as though seeing Jesus was just an everyday occurrence!

Throughout the years that one profound memory has served to give Renee a comfort and assurance that God is real, and it has placed within her the hope of being in His presence to assuage all things harsh in this world. I can say the same of my memory of meeting Jesus. God intentionally uses memories such as these for good. He designed our brains so that with repetition or a link to strong emotions, the connection between our brain cells (neurons) becomes stronger and stronger.[2]

This explains why repeating a verse over and over commits it to memory. And it explains why whenever you hear a song that you liked years ago, other events from the same time period can flood your mind. When you activate the neurons for that memory, related chunks of memories are activated as well. God uses this mechanism of the brain to confront trials as we place them in the context of having successfully persevered through them in the past.

As a trainer and coach, I have often encouraged those facing challenges to consider what they have overcome in the past to build confidence that they can do it again with the mentality of "been there, done that," which instills resiliency. I say something like this:

"Think of a time when you faced an obstacle that seemed insurmountable, and you got through it successfully. Do you remember a situation like this? Good, how did it make you feel? Strong? More confident? Surprised? Delighted? Okay, now take that problem or obstacle you are facing now. Place that obstacle in the same setting after you conquered that seemingly insurmountable obstacle you previously faced. Now, use that remembered position of strength as proof that you can do it again."

Try that exercise the next time you face a seemingly insurmountable obstacle. It really works. Remembering how God got you through the past provides evidence that He can do it for you again.

Each moment we live in the present reflects the light of the past as we strive to build the kinds of memories that will help us in the future. God used memories to help His children, as when He called the Israelites to remember all that He had done for them in the past: He defeated Pharaoh and delivered them from great trials. Today, He calls us to remember how He has helped us and will continue to be with us in the present. He will provide for our needs. And He will overcome the challenges that come our way. God uses memory to overcome trials by rekindling hope as testified by the past.

God Himself uses memory as a means to bless us. He spoke through the psalmist: "The Lord remembers us. He will bless us. He will bless the house of Israel. He will bless the house of Aaron" (Psalm 115:12 NHEB). When God remembered Rachel, He gave her a child (Genesis 30:22), and when He remembered Noah, the flood waters receded (see 8:1). Whenever God remembered His promise to Israel, He restored Israel just as He will restore you following your sufferings. Remembrance of what is good equates to healing when it comes to our trials. God remembers your faithfulness to Him and will bless you accordingly (see Hebrews 6:10).

Throughout our lives, God has renewed our minds to reconnect our brain's synapses to what is good and restorative (see Philippians 4:8; Colossians 3:2). This is why it is so important to meditate on what is good. God provided a Helper, the Holy Spirit. Jesus said the Spirit will teach us everything He said (John 14:26). Memories not only comfort us, but they direct us to our purpose in life.

Our purpose in the future is divinely connected to our past. Corrie ten Boom knew this. Corrie was a Dutch Christian who risked all to hide Jews from the Nazis during World War II (an awe-inspiring story recounted in *The Hiding Place*). In her book *In My Father's House*, which recounts the years before she became part of the Christian resistance, Corrie said this about the past and future: "Today I know that memories are the key not to the past, but to the future. I know that the experiences of our lives, when we let God use them, become the mysterious and perfect preparation for the work He will give us to do."[3]

If you find yourself haunted by some memories now, take consolation from the fact that God can heal you from them. Paradoxically, recalling troubling memories can actually help us heal old wounds. When we supplant those bad memories with God's promises, the Spirit of God assuages our hurts. For example, Jesus promises to give us His ultimate peace apart from anything that the world gives us (see John 14:27). First Peter 5:7 tells us that God cares for us, and that we can cast all our anxieties on Him. And Romans 8 promises that "in all things God works for the good of those who love him" (verse 28), and nothing can "separate us from the love of God" (verses 38–39). By remembering God's promises and accepting them as our present reality, we are renewing our minds (see Romans 12:2) apart from any harmful recollections.

When all else fails, remember that heaven is your true home. And given that reality, I thought it best to share with you my glimpses of heaven as I remembered them.

Glimpses of Heaven

After praying a lot about how best to conclude this book, I believe God's Spirit told me to share my glimpses of heaven. Now I know the "doubting Thomas" in some may challenge this account. But giving you a taste of heaven will perhaps prepare you to accept your death and eternal life, or the death of a loved one, with greater peace. I journaled my account in heaven, but for thirteen years I resisted sharing it publicly.

After meeting Jesus face-to-face and being discharged from the hospital, on several occasions the Holy Spirit brought to mind a freshness of my experiences in heaven. I would be reminded of my conversations with Jesus and the surroundings I witnessed in heaven. Before I share with you these glimpses of heaven, let's take a look at what the Bible says about the "heavens."

The Bible speaks of different heavens. Genesis 1:1 says God created "the heavens"—plural. The first heaven might be interpreted as the universe surrounding the earth. In describing the rain that brought on the flood in Noah's time, Genesis 7 says, "The windows of heaven were opened. . . . And all the high hills under the whole heaven were covered" (verses 11, 19 KJV). Now we come to the second heaven, which is the outer space, the universe (i.e., the region outside the earth where we find other planetary bodies).

The universe is not the heaven where we are destined to live with God; rather, it is a physical place described in the Bible. Exodus 32:13 is one of several references to "the stars of heaven." Stars are not in the skies (first heaven) from which the rain falls, but in a space beyond our atmosphere. Nehemiah 9:6 refers to heaven: "You alone are the LORD. You made the heavens, even the highest heavens, and all their starry host, the earth and all that is on it, the seas and all that is in them. You give life to everything, and the multitudes of heaven worship you."

Paul mentions the "third heaven" in 2 Corinthians 12:2, then "paradise" in verse 4.[4] *Paradise* is translated from the Greek word *paradeisos*, meaning "park" or "garden"—the same word used in *Garden of Eden* in the standard Greek translation of the Old Testament.[5] That place Paul described, not just any park or garden but a magnificent one, is more akin to the one I observed during my time with Jesus.

Perhaps another heaven exists where God almighty sits on His throne. I cannot say for sure. But I can tell you this: The paradise I visited was breathtakingly beautiful. I also remember that my attention was so focused on Jesus that I was inclined to ignore the beauty surrounding me. Being in Christ's presence is paradise in and of itself.

The Incomparable Joy of Meeting Jesus

On several occasions after my encounter with Jesus, the Holy Spirit compelled me to journal my observations as I lay dying in the hospital. At first, I fell into shock as a result of the "killer clot" in my lungs that was compounded by sepsis due to systemic infections. Then everything turned dark and my body started convulsing. Next, my body felt airy. I could hear people near my bed, but I was not in my bed, though I could faintly see my still body below.

I floated in a hazy space illuminated by light from above, a light I assumed was the sun. I looked over a mountain covered in mist with water drizzling over green slopes. *I dare not look up*, I thought, *or else I might be blinded by the intensity of the light.* Creatures I had never seen before battled each other in the distance. The pull from above kept me rising until the hills I had been observing faded into the distance. I found myself in a haze or mist that felt warm and refreshing. The warmth surpassed any creature comfort I had ever experienced in life.

That, my beloved friends, is where my account of meeting Jesus begins.

At that very moment, I felt comforted beyond belief. The light I'd witnessed had revealed Himself as Jesus Christ. My Savior tenderly embraced me. Yet I could not tell you exactly what I felt, since no words throughout the dialects of humankind could adequately explain it. How can one define pure love incarnate or the touch of consummate love?

When Jesus caressed me, He ripped away all of the cares that encumbered me. Everything drifted away like melted ice, leaving behind the snuggling feeling of a warm blanket on a cold night, and I snuggled with Him like a two-year-old formerly lost, now comforted by the most loving parent—a love that gives infinite rest.

Comfort—that word came to mind every time I looked into His eyes, the eyes of, shall I say, peace? I reposed upon His chest, which felt like a bed of roses. Roses—yes, that's what I smelled—wonderful floral smells that imparted assurance and peace. Time became irrelevant when I met Him in this place, this . . . heaven! In understated awe, I bowed down before Jesus Christ, wanting nothing but to please Him, worship Him, venerate Him with every fiber of my being. Oh, my!

I cannot even recount such adoration beyond mention . . . words made trite . . . abundant glory . . . magnificent in the extreme! I wanted to adore Him beyond my capacity to worship anyone, to reach beyond my limitations in allowing my reverence to burst forth in complete fullness made pale against what was truly owed my Lord! "Oh, my Lord! You are perfect in every way and so above my ability to worship You with any semblance of worthiness. Your majesty and power and glory are high above the highest praises! My Lord! Glory be the King of kings and Lord of lords! Holy is the Lamb of God, the Prince of Peace!" And then I broke down in tears, unable to control my wellspring of adulation.

Jesus reached down to softly lift me from my prostrate position. With tenderness, He wiped the tears running down my eyes, and as He did, an impartation of assurance consumed me. "I have been waiting for you, My beloved child," He first spoke to me.

I was overcome with breathless excitement and awe. I was so excited and giddy that my shaking would not stop. My lips quivered as I shook in awe of Jesus' absolute love. His presence exuded love! My entire body trembled like a dog after seeing his master return home.

I looked around to see rows of radiant stones or crystals—objects I had never seen before. They danced with the most brilliant colors, emitting effervescent light throughout that wondrous place. Paved roads—or rather pathways you might find through rolling hills—were spectacularly golden. They gave off a radiant glow resplendent with colors I'd never seen before. Everything glistened softly in light shades: the colors of velvety butterflies and cheerful flowers. Waves of hills and majestic mountains lay nested on some type of stream, which appeared like a flowing river—a long flowing river spread throughout the entire surroundings for as far as the eyes could behold.

Sparkling waters nourished everything; even the translucent rocks drank in the waters. These waters gave life, glorious life. Everything touched by the waters sprouted life, even the plants were growing before my eyes, sprouting flowers within seconds; even the translucent stones seemed to vibrate with some form of living presence. I noticed that the river flowed from Jesus Himself. What a spectacular sight!

"I feel at home," I said.

I did not want to return to the world. I had become so enthralled and embedded in this place of wonder. At no time in my wildest imagination could I fathom such beauty. It transcended my own thoughts, as the outward beauty seeped into every pore of my existence. Every part of heaven spoke peace and assurance. Life had never been so alive. I couldn't seem to do justice to anything I expressed. Anything less than the highest superlative would be inadequate, though no superlative could describe even the smallest particle in heaven. That paradise danced with joy. Even while I thought those words, I knew Jesus Christ was reading my mind.

"You are with Me always, My beloved," He responded. "I have known you from before you were born, in all ways and in all things." His words kept comforting me. Then, Jesus' hands touched me, filling me with assurance.

"So, you are Jesus and the Holy Spirit, my Lord?" I asked.

"When I speak to My children in the world, it is My Spirit that speaks. But all that I express is comfort. Nothing that I do or say should cause discomfort."

I wanted to stay with Jesus but knew that something else was planned. I knew Jesus understood what I was thinking, so I simply waited for His response.

"I am sending you back, My beloved. Many have prayed for you, and My purpose for you is not yet complete."

"But I have to go back? Please, no. I want to stay. This is home. Please!"

Jesus looked at me with His graceful, passionate eyes.

I did not want to go. Everything was so perfect, so—and there I thought again—comfortable.

There were other spirits going about their own activity. Some were magnificent, ten feet tall or so. They were fiercely resplendent, mighty to behold yet awesome to the point of commanding reverence. I knew, however, that only Jesus commanded my reverence. That much was absolutely clear.

Those like me, whose spirits traveled from the world to this place, appeared vibrant, youthful and full of joy. They glided along their way, occasionally dipping their hands into the running waters, sipping it, and each time they did, their countenance seemed to glow brighter than before.

I wanted to know more, but even more importantly, I wanted to just rest with my Lord. What was my purpose? I wondered.

"The life each lives on earth is a process of discovery, My beloved. My truth is imparted to those who know Me."

"But now I have to go back—to complete my purpose?" I felt like a little child waking up to meet Santa early Christmas morning only to be summoned back to his bedroom in the middle of the night.

I viewed a promenade with columns taller than I could see. From column to column hung lavish garments made of white fabric finer than silk. The same peace permeated the space all around me. Here, however, I sensed tremendous joy.

Figures frolicked through petals of soft linen that cushioned their feet as they walked. Angelic beings harmonized with worshipful music more grandiose, more awe-inspiring than anything in the world. The enchanting sounds exceeded twenty symphonies, accompanied by angelic voices lifting praises to "almighty God, Abba Father, Lord of Hosts, the Great I Am."

Joy exuded from every sight and sound, causing my heart to leap with excitement. Yet before I could leap effortlessly through meadows laced with flower petals, the now-familiar hand of my Lord pressed me into Him.

"You see My joy," Jesus said.

I guessed that the more you serve others unselfishly in the world, the greater your joy in heaven.

"Look downward, My beloved." Jesus looked more somber as He motioned to the world through a bubble-like window separating heaven from what we called earth. That world was really the world apart from God's fullness where I used to live. I could see multitudes of people going about their lives and gigantic spiritual warriors whispering or fighting or manifesting themselves in human forms.

I was hungry to know more, yet at the same time, I knew what was most important—being with the One who loved me most. I related to my Lord but not with a head knowledge; I simply knew, as in a genuine appreciation that all things were working for God's purpose—that He was in control—and that was enough.

"Your Kingdom, Lord, what is Your Kingdom?"

Jesus' eyes glistened with joy as He spoke. "My Kingdom is within each believer, and within Me, beloved. It is My impartation of who I am. The warfare you see is the fighting between My angels and those who have fallen, and My beloved who fight against these dark powers. My angels direct My beloved to me and when a person receives truth, he or she is freed to receive My impartation. The demons you see spread lies. They want to confuse My beloved so that they cannot hear the truth, and in so doing, they blind their victims to Me. Only My Spirit can be manifested in My children, and without My Spirit, people are dead to My Kingdom, My presence. The whisperers you see are messengers. My Spirit speaks truth, and the demons speak deceit and lies, seeking to confuse even the elect."

I knew that I would take my Lord's lessons back with me to the world to fulfill my purpose of bringing hope to the hopeless and sharing His truth, and to spread the joy of the Lord. The next question festering within me caused me to become anxious, as though I would insult Jesus by asking it. Yet I had to ask it!

"Dear Lord, why can You not reveal my purpose to me now?"

"My dear child, each person in the world must discover their purpose each day. If I were to reveal your purpose in full, leaving nothing to question, you would not rely upon Me. You would be tempted to accomplish your purpose without Me by relying on yourself instead of Me, seeking your ways and not Mine. Each of My creations in the world is created with purpose. The problem with My beloved is that they try to get ahead of My purpose, to do it according to their understanding apart from My leading. I desire, therefore, to keep My beloved dependent on Me within each moment. I know this frustrates many because they do not fully trust Me. You must trust Me and continually seek My revelation, however, so that you will not only know your purpose but also so that you will be empowered by My Spirit to fulfill your purpose."

It was all fitting in place now. My purpose would be revealed at the right time at the right place if only I would wait patiently on the Lord. And then, and only then, His power would enable me to fulfill His purpose. Hallelujah!

"So, the secret is in being, more than doing? More about getting close to You?"

I so loved that smile Jesus gave me when I was onto something deep. It was better than a warm fire on a freezing night. "My Spirit has revealed this to you, My beloved."

"How can I be who You want me to be in order to do what You want me to do?" I asked. A large butterfly tattooed in glowing colors of blue, green and orange settled on the back of my hand as if to signal the soft beauty that is wisdom, God's guiding light—or so I knew.

"Spend time with Me, beloved."

Sometimes the Lord's most profound answers came not in words but in the Spirit's tailored revelation to strike at the core of what I needed at that specific moment. Wisdom that came from fellowship with God would serve as my guide.

I understood that time with God was the key to my direction and strength. I could do nothing of value unless I stopped struggling to accomplish and started being present with God. The doing part was a by-product of being steeped in His presence.

The illuminating light that effused all of heaven began turning colors of orange mixed with purple and yellow and other brilliant colors I had never seen before—a kind of heavenly storm was underway. Only, this storm produced rains of refreshment intermixed with a hallowed sense of wonder. Beams of light also produced an increasing reverence for God, manufacturing an increasingly worshipful heart within me and others.

I felt like praising God with every facet of my being. Euphoria for my God overflowed; even the rivers and streams all throughout this glorious place began to overflow, flooding everywhere without drowning anything. The overflowing living waters produced an expanse of life. Every living thing cried out praises to God—even the rocks cried out![6]

Jesus came alongside me and whispered into my ear: "You must go now, but remember, I will never forsake you, My dearest one."

With this, I began to fall from my Lord's embrace, though His presence still lingered with the fresh scent of perfume so soothing and enlivening that I wished a stronger breath to breathe it in.

The Almighty I Am roared thunderously as I entered a space of limbo.

And then I heard the faint prayers of others releasing the commands of God in my situation—at least that's what I remember. These prayers seemed like cascading waterfalls from heaven to earth.

I floated in the space of nothingness with comforting ease. Though I wanted so much to return to heaven, I knew that I traveled with God's purpose instilled within me, ready to be borne out upon the earth. But oh, how I loved the comforting embrace of my Savior and wanted to stay.

Then it changed.

As if my purpose were pushing to be born, everything changed. Gone was the comforting embrace of my Father protecting me, and I found myself back in the harsh dryness of the world.

Most striking upon reawakening was, interestingly, the medicinal smell of disinfectant in the room—quite a contrast to the sweet fragrance in heaven. Pain shot through my back as I strained to breathe. Every muscle ached as I tried to force my eyes open.

Yet I remembered the songs of the angels—how beautiful the sound—and then this couple at my bedside were singing the same song of praises to God. So this is what I had heard: the sound of these two enjoined with a choir of angels.

It was time for me to go to work, "as unto the Lord" (Colossians 3:23 ASV). As the days and nights proceeded, I knew there would be suffering and trials. But always, always, joy would be around the corner.

In fact, I wrote the conclusion to this book while lying in the emergency room during one of several recent bouts with pneumonia and other issues. The hospital staff were very concerned, but not me. I knew that the worst that could happen in their eyes is the best that could happen to me.

Regardless of any suffering, the profoundest truth I have learned is that *nothing* compares to being in the presence of Jesus. Absolutely nothing. After all, heaven is in our future, and that is pretty doggone great. I know because I have been there.

Notes

Chapter 1 Face-to-Face

1. *Wikipedia*, s.v. "George Bailey (*It's a Wonderful Life*)," last modified June 30, 2019, https://en.wikipedia.org/wiki/George_Bailey_(It%27s_a _Wonderful_Life).

2. Matthew Henry, "Commentary on 2 Corinthians 12 by Matthew Henry," Blue Letter Bible, accessed July 9, 2019, https://www.blueletterbible .org/Comm/mhc/2Cr/2Cr_012.cfm.

Chapter 2 The Sadness

1. P. L. Strickland, J. F. W. Deakin, C. Percival, et al., "The Bio-Social Origins of Depression in the Community: Interactions between Social Adversity, Cortisol and Serotonin Neurotransmission," *British Journal of Psychiatry* 180 (2002): 168–173.

2. S. Killcross, T. W. Robbins, and B. J. Everitt, "Different Types of Fear-Conditioned Behaviour Mediated by Separate Nuclei within Amygdala," *Nature* 388, no. 6640 (1997): 377–80.

3. *Wikipedia*, s.v. "Footprints (poem)," last modified June 30, 2019, https:// en.wikipedia.org/wiki/Footprints_(poem).

4. Sean McDowell, *The Fate of the Apostles: Examining the Martyrdom Accounts of the Closest Followers of Jesus* (New York: Routledge, 2016).

Chapter 3 Walking with a Limp

1. Harvard Second Generation Study, http://adultdevelopment.wix.com/ harvardstudy.

Chapter 4 Finding Purpose through Pain

1. *Merriam-Webster's Dictionary*, s.v. "vocation," accessed July 9, 2019, http://www.merriam-webster.com/dictionary/vocation.

2. Randy Kay, *The Power to Thrive! Building the Foundations of a Thriving Career and Life* (Carlsbad: UpWord Media, 2018).

Chapter 5 Knowing God As a Friend

1. *Strong's Hebrew Lexicon* (NIV), s.v. "H6440—*paniym*," Blue Letter Bible, accessed June 20, 2019, https://www.blueletterbible.org//lang/lexicon/lexicon.cfm?Strongs=H6440&t=NIV.

2. *Strong's Greek Lexicon* (KJV), s.v. "G3841—pantokratōr," Blue Letter Bible, accessed June 20, 2019, https://www.blueletterbible.org//lang/lexicon/lexicon.cfm?Strongs=g3841&t=kjv.

3. J. M. Barrie, *Peter Pan*, quoted in Goodreads, "Peter Pan Quotes," accessed June 20, 2019, https://www.goodreads.com/quotes/tag/peter-pan.

Chapter 6 The Power

1. *Strong's Greek Lexicon* (NIV), s.v. "G3461—*myrias*," Blue Letter Bible, accessed June 20, 2019, https://www.blueletterbible.org//lang/lexicon/lexicon.cfm?Strongs=G3461&t=NIV.

2. Like the Master Ministries, "How Many Angels Are There?," Never-Thirsty, accessed June 20, 2019, https://www.neverthirsty.org/bible-qa/qa-archives/question/how-many-angels-are-there/.

3. *Wikipedia*, s.v. "List of Largest Cities," last modified June 25, 2019, https://en.wikipedia.org/wiki/List_of_largest_cities.

4. Karel van der Toorn, Bob Becking, and Pieter W. van der Horst, eds., "Demon," *Dictionary of Deities and Demons in the Bible*, 2nd ed. (Grand Rapids: William B. Eerdmans, 1999), 235–240.

Chapter 7 Dying to Self

1. Aaron Bicknese, *The Teen Challenge Drug Treatment Program in Comparative Perspective* (Evanston: Northwestern University, 1999).

2. Association of Christian Alcohol & Drug Counselors (ACADC), "Significant Research That Everybody Should Know," February 21, 2009.

3. Burk Parsons, "Immanuel," *Tabletalk*, December 5, 2017, https://tabletalkmagazine.com/article/2017/12/immanuel-temple/.

4. *Strong's Greek Lexicon* (NIV), s.v. "G4637—*skēnoō*," Blue Letter Bible, accessed June 20, 2019, https://www.blueletterbible.org//lang/lexicon/lexicon.cfm?Strongs=G4637&t=niv.

5. *Strong's Greek Lexicon* (NIV), s.v. "G3076—*lypeō*," Blue Letter Bible, accessed June 19, 2019, https://www.blueletterbible.org//lang/lexicon/lexicon.cfm?Strongs=G3076&t=NIV.

6. Hersh Goldwurm, "Appendix: Year of the Destruction," *History of the Jewish People: The Second Temple Era* (Brooklyn: Mesorah Publications, 1982).

Chapter 8 Dying to Meet Jesus

1. K. S. LaBar and R. Cabeza, "Cognitive Neuroscience of Emotional Memory," *Nature Reviews Neuroscience* 7, no. 1 (2006): 54–64.

2. David A. DeWitt, "What Memories Are Made Of," Answers in Genesis, May 28, 2018, https://answersingenesis.org/human-body/brain/what-memories-are-made-of/.

3. Corrie ten Boom, quoted in "Corrie ten Boom Quotes," Goodreads, accessed June 20, 2019, https://www.goodreads.com/author/quotes/102203 .Corrie_ten_Boom?page=8.

4. For a comprehensive study of heaven, see 2 Corinthians 12 in Matthew Henry, *Acts to Revelation*, vol. 4 of *Commentary on the Whole Bible*, Christian Classics Ethereal Library, https://www.ccel.org/ccel/henry/mhc6.html.

5. *Strong's Greek Lexicon* (NIV), s.v. "G3857—*paradeisos*," accessed June 19, 2019, https://www.blueletterbible.org//lang/lexicon/lexicon.cfm?Strongs =G3857&t=NIV.

6. See Luke 19:39–40.

Randy Kay is the Chief Learning Officer for PACEsetters, a human development firm specializing in thriving mindsets, leadership, social intelligence and coaching. He is an ordained minister who has taught courses throughout the world to Christian audiences and has been a CEO or board member for eleven Christian and philanthropic organizations. He has been a biotech/medtech CEO, executive for Fortune 100 companies, entrepreneur in starting four companies and board member for over twenty organizations, and he is clinically trained in cardiovascular surgery and neurology.

Kay has authored three nonfiction books—*Daily Keys to Success*, *The Power to Thrive* and *The 22 Most Important Things*. His articles have been read in major publications such as *Forbes*, *Switch & Shift* and others, and he has been interviewed on numerous stations throughout the United States such as GodTV, during which he first shared his near-death experience (NDE) in a large public forum.